This is a terrific message from a trusted .... to endorse it. Families will be encouraged, instructed, and empowered!

Max Lucado
Pastor and Best-Selling Author

. . . .

I know of no one with a greater understanding of how to reach the hearts of little ones than Jean. She embraces this as a high calling and the fruit she has to share will enrich your life.

Sheila Walsh
Author, Recording Artist,
Speaker (Women of Faith)

. . . .

It's about time! I have been after Jean Thomason to write a book for parents for years! For most of my life, parents have looked to the church to teach their kids to be worshipers of the one true God. But the church can't do this alone. The church needs a partner, and there is no better partner than the persons God chose in the beginning to be the primary spiritual caregivers of their children, parents! (Read Deuteronomy 6:4–8). This book will give you the skills to be the parents your kids need so they can be who God has created them to be. Great job, Cake—you nailed it! I am so excited that the wisdom you have shared at conferences and the truths you have walked out with your own dear children will now be available to parents every-where. Don't just read this, Mom and Dad—do it!

Jim Wideman
NextGen and Children's Ministry Pioneer,
Author, Coach, and Consultant
Jim Wideman Ministries, Inc.
www.jimwideman.com

· ·

Miss PattyCake is an amazing teacher/entertainer/worship leader for preschool children! This same talent for connecting with people comes through very clearly in her new book, *Sharing God's Big Love with Little Lives*. Her years of fun experiences make a very entertaining read for anyone interested in preschool children. Every new parent who is interested in training up children in the ways they should go should read this book. Jean is a shining example of a woman who has followed God's call on her life and has done amazing things. Her influence will live on for many years to come through her songs, her DVDs, and now through the wise and funny words in her new book. Congratulations, Jean, on letting your light shine for Him!

Dr. Beth Watkins Cape
Director of Preschool Ministries
Whitesburg Baptist Church
Huntsville, Alabama

· ·

Miss PattyCake rocked my world. I was just your typical, run-of-the-mill, spandex-clad, purple-cape-toting, full-armor-of-God-wearing, Bible-based superhero, husband, and father when the jolly green jewel of preschool ministry infiltrated our family in the most amazing ways.

I'll never forget the night my wife and I pulled the pink princess sheets onto our toddling daughter's bed. We knew in an instant that her decision to kneel down with hands clasped and head bowed was inspired by Miss PattyCake's song that echoed throughout our home: "Thank You, thank You, Jesus. Thank You. Thank You." My little princess chose to thank Jesus for her big-girl bed.

A few years later—after deciding to stop wearing spandex in public—I saw my preschool-aged son rush to the lobby of the church I pastored in Colorado. He wanted to greet the people as they arrived. Zachary welcomed all his friends, young and old, as they entered to worship. Over and over, I could hear the giggling voice of Miss PattyCake as he shouted, "My friends are here!"

Now Miss PattyCake has done it again. Jean Thomason has once more listened to the voice of our Savior and obediently agreed to offer biblically-based wisdom to parents of preschoolers as only Miss PattyCake can.

Sharing God's Big Love with Little Lives builds on the wealth of experience and wisdom Jean has absorbed through decades of parenting and partnering with the Holy Spirit to speak into the lives of families with preschoolers. Miss PattyCake has always offered much more than preschool entertainment with a Christian worldview. Miss PattyCake is a friend to parents who wants to help us fulfill the greatest calling imaginable: "Start children off on the way they should go, and even when they are old they will not turn from it" (Proverbs 22:6).

Robert T. Schlipp
Pastor, Evangelist, Former Superhero
(Bibleman: 2003–2011)

. . . .

I love the book! Love the title, love the scriptural light woven throughout, love the dedication, love, love the chapters and the significance of each! So clever, well done, and encouraging! Such an excellent work, Jean!

Sherri Moore
Friend, Social Worker, Mother of Four

Over the past several years I have worked in three different churches, and Miss PattyCake has ministered to preschoolers and their parents at each church. Her laughter is contagious, and parents are encouraged by her words of deep, godly wisdom as she shares through her gifts of speaking and music. This book is a must-read for anyone with preschoolers in their lives.

Stacy Holman
Minister to Preschoolers and Children
First Baptist Church
Albany, Georgia

SHARING GOD'S
BIG L♥VE
with
LITTLE LIVES

SHARING GOD'S BIG LVE with LITTLE LIVES

A Can-Do Guide for Parents and Caregivers

Jean Thomason

WORTHY®
PUBLISHING

Copyright © 2017 by Jean Thomason

Published by Worthy Books, an imprint of Worthy Publishing Group, a division of Worthy Media, Inc., One Franklin Park, 6100 Tower Circle, Suite 210, Franklin, TN 37067.

WORTHY is a registered trademark of Worthy Media, Inc.

HELPING PEOPLE EXPERIENCE THE HEART OF GOD

Library of Congress Control Number: 2017931622

All rights reserved. No portion of this book may be reproduced, stored in a retrieval system, or transmitted in any form or by any means—electronic, mechanical, photocopy, recording, scanning, or other—except for brief quotations in critical reviews or articles, without the prior written permission of the publisher.

All Scripture quotations, unless otherwise indicated, are taken from the Holy Bible, New International Version®, NIV®. Copyright © 1973, 1978, 1984, 2011 by Biblica, Inc™. Used by permission of Zondervan. All rights reserved worldwide. | Scripture quotations marked KJV are taken from the King James Version of the Bible. Public domain. | Scripture quotations marked NKJV are taken from the New King James Version®. Copyright © 1982 by Thomas Nelson. Used by permission. All rights reserved. | Scripture quotations marked NASB are taken from the New American Standard Bible®, Copyright © 1960, 1962, 1963, 1968, 1971, 1972, 1973, 1975, 1977, 1995 by The Lockman Foundation. Used by permission. (www.Lockman.org) | Scripture quotations marked AMP are taken from the Amplified® Bible, Copyright © 2015 by The Lockman Foundation, La Habra, CA 90631. All rights reserved. | Scripture quotations marked MSG are taken from The Message. Copyright 1993, 1994, 1995, 1996, 2000, 2001, 2002. Used by permission of NavPress Publishing Group. | Scripture quotations marked ESV are taken from the ESV® Bible (The Holy Bible, English Standard Version®), copyright © 2001 by Crossway, a publishing ministry of Good News Publishers. Used by permission. All rights reserved. | Scripture quotations marked NET are taken from the New English Translation®, NET Bible®. Copyright © 1996-2006 by Biblical Studies Press, L.L.C. Used by permission. All rights reserved. (www.netbible.com) | Scripture quotations marked NLT are taken from the Holy Bible, New Living Translation, copyright © 1996, 2004, 2007 by Tyndale House Foundation. Used by permission of Tyndale House Publishers, Inc., Carol Stream, Illinois 60188. All rights reserved. | Scripture quotations marked GW are taken from GOD'S WORD®, © 1995 God's Word to the Nations. Used by permission of Baker Publishing Group.

For foreign and subsidiary rights, contact rights@worthypublishing.com

eBook available wherever digital books are sold.

ISBN: 978-1-61795-862-5 (paperback)

Cover Design: Marc Whitaker, MTW Design
Interior Design and Typesetting: Bart Dawson

Printed in the United States of America
17 18 19 20 21 LBM 8 7 6 5 4 3 2 1

CONTENTS

This book is dedicated to you, dear reader,
because you are taking time to better equip yourself
as you speak into little lives. You are obeying God.
This effort matters for eternity.

INTRODUCTION

This is the day the LORD has made;
we will rejoice and be glad in it.

PSALM 118:24 (NKJV)

Psalm 118:24 is a verse I have known as long as I can remember (thanks, Mom)! I quote it, I sing it, I use it to encourage my children, I speak it over negative or frustrating circumstances, I open every concert and every speaking opportunity with it, and it is the quintessential Jean/Miss PattyCake verse. I love proclaiming God as the Maker in those words, and the fun of rejoicing and being glad! Often I say it offhandedly and forget the power of that verse—especially the two words "we will." We will—meaning we choose. It's a verb—something we *do*. For me, that is the beginning of understanding praise to God. Every day it is *my choice* to give thanks and praise to God.

So I practice praise and recite this verse. And it works for me. But what about my little children? How do I teach them to "rejoice and be glad"? All of us parents, grandparents, and caregivers know we need help to do that.

I start with my preschool paraphrase:

EVERY DAY IS A PATTYCAKE PRAISE DAY!

Many of you who know me as Miss PattyCake have heard me (her) say this paraphrased verse. If you watch the DVDs or listen to the CDs, I hope your children repeat it *ad absurdum*! Because "it is *good* to give thanks to the Lord, and to sing praises to Your name" (Psalm 92:1 NKJV, emphasis mine).

The character we now call Miss PattyCake was originally called PattyCake Praise, and she was created to teach children to praise God. The catalyst for this character was a song called "PattyCake Praise," which was an effort to use the old "pat-a-cake" nursery rhyme together with Psalm 47:1 (AMP), which instructs us:

> *Clap your hands, all you people;*
> *Shout to God with the voice of triumph*
> *and songs of joy.*

The "PattyCake Praise" song, written by Nancy Gordon and Chris Springer, says:

> *Pattycake, pattycake, clap and play.*
> *Pattycake, pattycake, every day.*
> *Pattycake, pattycake, praise the Lord.*
> *Pattycake, pattycake, praise!*[1]

Those lyrics along with the words of the psalm fueled the idea for a fun, colorful, musical, costumed friend/teacher. This character would sing songs to teach Bible stories, praise, and early educational games. Songs, along with activities containing a biblical worldview, both designed to be fun for little ones, would be the mission. She would help parents, caregivers, and teachers use age-appropriate teaching tools centering on God who made us and who loves us, and who sent Jesus, His one and only Son, to live, die, and live again so we can be in His family forever.

WHEW! I know—big job, right? The scriptures already encourage us that little children can easily and naturally give praise to God:

> *Nursing infants gurgle choruses about you;*
> *toddlers shout the songs that drown out enemy talk,*
> *and silence atheistic babble.*
>
> PSALM 8:2 [MSG]

When I read that verse, it was as if I heard God say, *So, who is going to teach those songs to infants and toddlers?* I decided to give the answer Isaiah gave when he saw the Lord and heard a similar question: "'Whom shall I send? And who will go for us?' And I said, 'Here am I. Send me!'" (Isaiah 6:8).

When you say yes to God, He will take you seriously, send you out, and you'll never know exactly where you will go or what you will look like. For more than twenty years, I have been dressed in a kelly-green jumper with two hands and one heart appliquéd on three pockets over a striped or polka-dot blouse, tights, Mary Janes over bobby socks, and a fun hat with a big bow or flower sticking out of it. Some may think this is silly, but I remind myself of 1 Corinthians 1:25: "The foolishness of God is wiser than human wisdom." For these last two decades, it has pleased God to use the "foolishness" of a costumed character to communicate His love and truth through music to hundreds of thousands of children!

Praising God is a game changer. When I began to practice praising God it radically changed my life. If you will practice praise by yourself as well as with your children, and do it often, it *will* change you. It will change the way you deal with your circumstances, and it will change the atmosphere in your home, and that will affect all your relationships. Because I have experienced the power of praise and the change it makes in the lives of adults and children, I have chosen the word *praise* to be your guide in this handbook of help.

> Because I have experienced the power of praise and the change it makes in the lives of adults and children, I have chosen the word *praise* to be your guide in this handbook of help.

By using the letters of the word as the acronym *PRAISE*, this book will take you on a tour of parenting and teaching young children about our Lord and Savior. It will help you in the great work of spiritual formation, which is the joy of laying a biblical, spiritual foundation on which salvation and a life of faith can be built. Of course we cannot do this without the supernatural help of God, who is at work in and through us. This book is a can-do guide because you and I **can do** this job, with God helping us. Repeat after me, "I *can do* all things through Christ who strengthens me" (Philippians 4:13 NKJV, emphasis mine).

This book will refresh your belief that God has put a child or children in your life on purpose. He has given you everything you need to speak into this little life or lives as His ambassador, representing His kingdom. It is no mistake you are a parent, grandparent, teacher, or caregiver of a little child. It is a great responsibility, a privilege, and it can be a pleasure! These days go by more quickly than we think they will, so be wise and do not miss any opportunity to talk to children about God.

As we ask for help, God will equip us and give us wisdom. God is rejoicing over us with singing (see Zephaniah 3:17)! We will talk a lot about singing and many other ways to give God praise. Laughing with enthusiastic enjoyment is a big piece of the parenting puzzle, and I hope you get the giggles as you read this can-do guide. You can have joy in this journey, enjoying Him and enjoying your little one(s).

So, as Miss PattyCake always says, "With two hands to clap, one heart to love, and a voice to sing, every song can give thanks and praise to God, and we can make every day a PattyCake praise day!" Now take my hand and turn the page to begin the tour.

Chapter 1

PLACED AND PRIVILEGED TO PARENT

Behold, children are a gift of the LORD,
The fruit of the womb is a reward.

PSALM 127:3 [NASB]

ongratulations! You have won the prize! You get the reward: the incredible opportunity to love, protect, care for, and help shape a new life. WOW! That's . . . terrifying.

When we brought home our tiny first baby, I was giddy! My husband and I were enamored with that little blond girl with the loud voice. She was my dream come true. For me, pregnancy and delivery had been a lovely experience. I had never felt better in my life during those nine months and that epidural was the bomb! I was made for birthin' babies! I had lots of help in those early weeks: my mom came, as did my mother-in-law, my sister, and some friends. They cooked and cleaned and held the baby, and I slept and nursed.

It was all dreamy . . . for a while.

Then they all left.

My husband went to work and left me home—alone—with that tiny, screaming, eating machine. If I hadn't had a phone I may not be here today. Every day I called my mother. Every other day I called my best friend, who had her baby four weeks earlier, and we talked each other off the cliffs. I devoured every page of the baby books I had, read my Bible, prayed a lot, and slept little. In those days, I did *not* feel I had won a prize. I felt as if I were running a marathon without training!

I had heard horror stories of what might happen and believed them. The what-ifs threatened to keep me awake at night.

Every little sound—or lack of sound—sent me rushing into her room. I listened to the voice in my head: *What was I thinking? I can't do this! I am going to be a terrible mother! I am not sure I even LIKE children!*

When these lies and fears assaulted me, I prayed a one-word prayer: HELP! I knew I had to change my *stinking thinking.* Without fail, the Holy Spirit, in His kindness and brilliance, would drop a truth into my head, such as:

> *His divine power has given us*
> *everything we need for a godly life.*
>
> 2 PETER 1:3

. . . .

> *When I am afraid, I put my trust in you.*
>
> PSALM 56:3

. . . .

> *We take captive every thought*
> *to make it obedient to Christ.*
>
> 2 CORINTHIANS 10:5

The living Word of God is our best defense against the lies in our heads. Just remember where those lying thoughts originate— Satan. Also remind yourself that when Jesus was tempted by that liar, the only words He spoke began, "It is written . . ." (Luke 4:4). Jesus knew God's Word is "alive and active" (Hebrews 4:12), which gave Him strength against the onslaught of "the father of lies" (John 8:44).

You and I have that same weapon against lies, fears, doubts, and other sordid condemnation. I encourage you to arm yourself with these verses as you walk through your day and declare them. Say them out loud to any ears that may be listening. I wrote them on sticky notes and put them on my mirror and above my kitchen sink. I reminded myself, *God doesn't make mistakes! I was sovereignly, carefully chosen to be this child's mother.*

> "I am not alone.
> God is with me.
> He is my help.
> I can trust Him."

God is waiting for us to ask for His help! Jesus said, "Here I am! I stand at the door and knock. If anyone hears my voice and opens the door, I will come in" (Revelation 3:20).

> *The Lord longs to be gracious to you, and therefore He waits on high to have compassion.*
> ISAIAH 30:18 [NASB]

The New Living translation expands this verse and I think it is even more personal:

> *So the Lord must wait for you to come to him so he can show you his love and compassion. For the Lord is a faithful God. Blessed are those who wait for his help.*

After reading these scriptures, you should take a long, relaxing breath. There . . . better? No matter where you are in this journey of caring for children, these words from God can give you rest and peace. You can say these words over and over, "I am not alone. God is with me. He is my help. I can trust Him."

We have help from Father God and from others on this journey. Their prayers and encouragement are reassuring. I found more help when I came across the book *Soul Retreat for Moms* compiled by Lila Empson. I especially loved this particular passage written by my friend, Melinda Mahand:

Choose to take God's hand and join your heart with his. Just as a toddling child becomes more and more sure of his steps as he holds a parent's hand, so your steps will become firm as you walk with the Lord. He will meet all your needs, and you will experience the incredible reality that you are not alone. Today the Lord is offering to take your hand and walk beside you on life's journey. He wants to be not only your companion, but your guide and protector as well. Although you may be hurt by an occasional stumble, you will not be destroyed by a headlong fall as long as you are walking hand in hand with Him.[1]

GRADUATING

Will you indulge me as I share a bit more about my journey? When my children were one and two (sixteen months apart), I was looking for creative ways to talk to them about spiritual things—ways that were developmentally appropriate. I knew children respond much better to music than to spoken words.

Singing is a common occurrence in my house. I sing all day about anything and everything; I use hymns and praise songs around the house **a lot**. One day I was encouraging my three-year-old daughter, Marilyn, to sing along with me, "He is exalted, the King is exalted on high" from the song "He Is Exalted" by Twila Paris.[2] A bit confused, she looked up at me and asked, "Mommy, why is God so tired?" Something was lost in translation—she thought God was exhausted! That was the day I realized I needed new songs.

New songs and a big idea came from another mother, Nancy Gordon. It was her vision to create a costumed character who would sing Bible songs, praise songs, wiggly-giggly songs, and songs that teach colors, numbers, and the ABCs—sort of *Sesame Street* goes to Sunday school. Nancy and I took a few already recorded songs she and others had written, wrote a little story about a treasure chest from God, had a green jumper made with two hands and one heart on the pockets, and—voilà! Miss PattyCake was born. The very first time Miss PattyCake sang for mommies with their children was at the Mothers of Preschoolers (MOPS) meeting at Dauphin Way Baptist Church in Mobile, Alabama.

It was the children's pastor who said, "Jean, this is a really big idea! There is a huge need for music ministry to toddlers and preschoolers." That was sobering and challenging. I thought, *Well then, I'll do it!* I made some calls and started traveling, singing for little ones and parents in churches, schools, festivals, conferences, even a private birthday party in Paris, France . . . and I still am!

During my early years of parenting and Miss PattyCake "praising," I had the fabulous privilege of singing on the worship team for the Women of Faith conferences, which traveled to cities all over the country. I loved every minute of it. For almost ten years I took part in this ministry, and during those years the Miss PattyCake opportunities increased.

It was clear God had a big plan for Miss PattyCake as I got busier and busier with children's ministry. I knew it was time for me to step down from adult worship with Women of Faith to sing for children. It felt that way—like stepping down from a big stage in front of "big" people. I knew many women could take my place and sing on that stage, but very few were singing to little children. I wasn't really happy about this. I loved the women I worked with, I loved traveling and singing, and as we say in Nashville, it was a "great gig." Then came the day when my husband said, "Sweetie, I think you are done with Women of Faith." I gave my Isaiah 6:8 answer, "Here am I. Send me!" And I have been exclusively working with little ones and their parents ever since.

> God's ways are not our ways. In fact, they are often just the opposite.

I am not sure how you sense God's direction. It may be a Bible verse that seems to keep popping up, a heaviness or sense of unease, a nagging thought, advice from more than one trusted friend, or an aha moment. My conversation with God went this way: "All right, I get it, Lord. I know how serious You are about children, and I do love this 'kid gig.' So I thank You for where You are taking Miss PattyCake, and I will step down to sing for the children." And unexpectedly these words plopped into my mind: *No, no, you are not stepping down. You are stepping up! You have GRADUATED.*

Graduated? Really? Then it suddenly made sense. I remembered that the Bible teaches God's kingdom is upside down! God's ways are not our ways. In fact, they are often just the opposite. Jesus talked about this frequently. He said, "If you want to save your life, lose it," "Don't repay evil for evil," "The first will be the last," and "The least are greatest." (See Luke 17:33; 1 Peter 3:9; Matthew 20:16; Luke 9:48). And who did Jesus say were among the greatest? That's right—little children!

GOD'S KINGDOM IS UPSIDE DOWN

"In the upside-down kingdom of heaven,
down is up and up is down, and those
who want to ascend higher must descend lower.
And so 'anyone who becomes as humble
as this little child is the greatest in the Kingdom
of Heaven.' (Matthew 18:4 NLT)."

ANN VOSKAMP[3]

Other words spoken by Jesus confirm the truth that the least is the greatest in the kingdom and are found all through the gospels. Here are just a few of them:

Matthew 19:13-15	Mark 10:13-16
Matthew 20:26	Mark 10:43
Mark 9:35	Luke 18:15-17

I love the way F. B. Meyer speaks of the biblical concept of the upside-down kingdom:

I used to think that God's gifts were on shelves one above the other, and that the taller we grew in Christian character the easier we should reach them. I find now that God's gifts are on shelves one beneath the other, and that it is not a question of growing taller but of stooping lower, and that we have to go down, always down, to get His best gifts.[4]

Our Father has given us (parents, grandparents, teachers, caregivers) the enormous **privilege** and responsibility to teach and train little ones. And He has provided us with all the resources we need: His Word, the Holy Spirit who is with us, and the wise counsel of the trusted family of God. As you work this field, planting seeds in little lives, take heart! This *is* the high calling of God. It *is* His gift. It *is* an upgrade. The process of parenting will take you to a new place in your own relationship with Him. You have been placed and privileged to parent.

ENJOY YOUR REWARD!
(Don't be surprised when you realize you are actually having fun!)

Chapter 2

RARE WINDOW OF OPPORTUNITY

Teach us to number our days,
that we may gain a heart of wisdom.

PSALM 90:12

These first few years of your child's life are a sacred space. They form the foundation for the rest of his or her life. Those of us who care for children during this time have the rare opportunity to participate in this formation. At this stage, little children have the greatest capacity for learning. One of my favorite creative parenting books, *The Artist's Way for Parents* by Julia Cameron, puts it into perspective: "Parenting is also a spiritual undertaking. We are entrusted with the care of our children's souls as well as their bodies. . . . The early years of parenting can be one of the most inspiring chapters of your life, opening you to love and growth you may not have yet experienced."[1] Our job, in addition to keeping them alive and well, is helping them learn the big love story of the Bible so they will have a strong foundation of God's truth, which will help them come to know and live for Him.

These little ones are not only precious to us, but also to God. So much so that Jesus said of them in Matthew 18:10, **"See that you do not despise one of these little ones. For I tell you that their angels in heaven always see the face of my Father in heaven."** Jesus sternly rebuked His followers for keeping the children away from Him: "Let the little children come to me, and do not hinder them, for the kingdom of heaven belongs to such as these" (Matthew 19:14). Jesus identified little ones as part of His kingdom by blessing them. The term "bless" means "to show favor."[2] Jesus had great affection for these little ones and He folded them into His arms to touch and pray for them. It is clear throughout the scriptures that children have a special place. Do you know the old Sunday school song, "Jesus Loves the Little Children"?

Jesus loves the little children,
All the children of the world.
Red and yellow,
Black and white,
They are precious in His sight,
Jesus loves the little children of the world.[3]

We know God has **big love to share with little lives**. We know we are responsible, with God's help, for their spiritual formation. We must do nothing to "hinder them," as Jesus said. So how can we prepare for the task at hand?

UNDERSTAND THE TIMES

If you've read much of the Old Testament, you may be aware of the twelve tribes of Israel. These were the sons of Jacob who multiplied to become the Hebrew nation. Before Moses died, he spoke a prophetic blessing over each of the tribes. These blessings were God's gifts, equipping His people for the good of the nation (see Deuteronomy 33). One of the tribes named after Jacob's son, Issachar, had a unique spiritual gift— understanding the political and cultural times of the people. Here is a description of their spiritual insight: "From Issachar, men who understood the times and knew what Israel should do" (1 Chronicles 12:32). This gift was vitally important in the life of the nation of Israel. They needed wisdom and direction then just as we do now. Pastor Dave Whitehead from Grace Church in New York City brings this powerful idea into modern times:

> The writer of Chronicles makes a unique observation of the men of Issachar—they understood the times and knew what Israel should do. What an amazing skill! The world is constantly changing. Are we holding on to the "old ways of doing things" or are we taking the time to understand the ways that our communities are changing? This is the challenge of the church in the 21st Century—to not only understand the times, but also to know what to do.[4]

You may think this is an odd scripture reference, but I was captured by a sense of urgency when I discovered it. So much so I bought a necklace with a pocket watch hanging on a long chain, and I wear it often just to remind myself to "understand the times." Being aware of the culture, knowing what our children are facing in their future is paramount for us as leaders, teachers, parents, and grandparents as we work to teach them about God and His great big world.

The Bible speaks again of this same urgency in 1 Peter 5:8–9 (MSG): "Keep a cool head. Stay alert. The Devil is poised to pounce, and would like

We have a few very short years to help shape the little lives in our care.

nothing better than to catch you napping. Keep your guard up. You're not the only ones plunged into these hard times. It's the same with Christians all over the world. So keep a firm grip on the faith."

We have a few very short years to help shape the little lives in our care.

REALITY CHECK

When visiting Sherwood Baptist church in Albany, Georgia, I came across a sign in huge letters saying, "Whoever wants the next generation the most will get them." I thought, *Yes! Here is a group of people who gets it!* This statement happens to be one of the core values of that church. If you have worked long with little children or have studied much about early childhood education and development, you will understand why this is so very important.

> "Whoever wants the next generation the most will get them."

Ask yourself this question: *Who, in our culture, wants the next generation?* There are many answers. Think of all that competes for the attention of children: art, education, sports, dance, movies, the Internet. These are not all bad, but many are God-less. Even if we make the excellent effort of getting our children to church on a regular basis, the hours spent there add up to maybe fifty in a year. But moms and dads get between two thousand and three thousand flexible hours in the home every year. As parents, grandparents, or caregivers, you and I have all the time we need to talk to our children about God.

. . . .

If we don't teach our children who God is,
someone else will teach them
everything that He isn't.

DARLENE SCHACHT[5]

. . . .

After two years of researching child development and children's ministry, author and pollster George Barna said this:

When it comes to grasping the substance, the subtleties and the implications of the Christian faith, don't adults possess the greatest learning and intellectual capacities? Strategically, isn't it more important for us to equip adults so that they can use their gifts and resources to advance the Kingdom? No, no, no and no. In retrospect, my view was so far off the mark that not only have I missed the boat—I missed the entire ocean! Ministry to children is the single most important work in the Kingdom of God. And even more to the point, the most significant aspect of every person's life is his or her spiritual health. . . . Every dimension of a person's experience hinges on his or her moral and spiritual condition.[6]

Here are the findings of the Barna Group (and these are from 2004):

- Eighty-five percent of all born-again believers came to salvation by eight years of age.
- By the age of nine, most of the moral and spiritual foundations of a child are in place.
- A child's character is almost fully formed by age six.[7]

I was stunned when I first read these statistics. By the time I knew these to be true, I had been working with churches as Miss PattyCake for years and occasionally bumping into the mind-set that said, "Oh, just give them some crayons and paper, sing some little songs, feed them some crackers. When they get older and can understand, *then* we will share the gospel."

No, no, no, noooo—do not wait! **Do it now**. Talk, sing, and read to your children about God, even before you think they can understand the words. (We'll delve into this more in chapter 4.)

BRAINWASHING

One day after a Miss PattyCake concert a woman stopped me and asked, "Don't you feel you are brainwashing these children?"

Hmmmmm. I thought for a few seconds and said, "Yes! That's our *job*." And not just any brainwashing, but washing with the water of the Word of God (Ephesians 5:26). We can sing, read, and teach our little ones from the Bible, trusting God will use His living Word to work where we can't see. It is an underground activity. My friend Ginnie Johnson calls it "secret gardening."

> Talk, sing, and read to your children about God, even before you think they can understand the words.

There are mountains of research on the subject of infant brain development, early imprinting, physical, psychological, and emotional development from conception to birth and beyond. The numerous studies available would take years to read and process. I am sharing just a few quotes to help underscore the importance of this window of opportunity.

The earliest messages that the brain receives have an enormous impact. Imprinting takes place early. Early brain development is the foundation of human adaptability and resilience, but these qualities come at a price. Because experiences have such a great potential to affect brain development, children are especially vulnerable to persistent negative influences during this period. On the other hand, these early years are a *window of opportunity* for parents, caregivers, and communities: positive early experiences have a huge effect on children's chances for achievement, success, and happiness.

—Urban Child Institute[8]

The first three years of life are a period of incredible growth in all areas of a baby's development. A newborn's brain is about 25 percent of its approximate adult weight. But by age 3, it has grown dramatically by producing billions of cells and hundreds of trillions of connections, or synapses, between these cells. While we know that the development of a young child's brain takes years to complete, we also know there are many things parents and caregivers can do to help children get off to a good start and establish healthy patterns for life-long learning.

—Zero to Three: National Center for Infants,
Toddlers and Families[9]

For a number of reasons, the two years leading to the fifth birthday are a unique and critical period during which you can shape the entire gamut of your child's attitudes and understanding. . . . Whether the topic is animals, trucks, the color of the sky, or the attributes of God, he will be all ears (even though his mouth may seem to be in perpetual motion) and deeply concerned about what you think. This wide-eyed openness will not last forever. While you will greatly influence his thinking throughout childhood, during the coming months you will have an important *window of opportunity* to lay foundations that will affect the rest of his life. No one can do this job perfectly; therefore generous doses of humility and much time in prayer are definitely in order for this phase of parenting.

Adapted from *Complete Guide
to Baby & Child Care*[10]

R. S. Lee, the author of *Your Growing Children and Religion*, says it this way: "The first seven years [of life] constitute the period for laying the foundations of religion. This is the most important period in the whole of a person's life in determining his later religious attitudes."[11]

Saint Ignatius of Loyola said in AD 1539:

Give me a child until he is seven, and I will show you the man.[12]

. . . .

The research is very clear: if Jesus is not already part
of their lives by the time they leave junior high school,
the chances of them accepting Him as their Lord
and Savior [are] very slim (6%, to be exact).
With children, it is just the opposite.
The greatest evangelical window currently available
is among young children.

GEORGE BARNA[13]

. . . .

Research has clearly substantiated the Bible verse, "Train up a child in the way he should go, and when he is old he will not depart from it" (Proverbs 22:6 NKJV). So go ahead and do what's best for your children by brainwashing them!

JELL-O

One day when my children were little, I took them on a field trip to the mall. Anything to get them out of the house and me out of the mess! Does that sound familiar? Well, on this day I saw something I will never forget. One of the ads along the walk-way caught my attention. It pictured a tiered Jell-O mold, bright green, with a large goldfish in the middle. The caption said:

A CHILD'S MIND IS LIKE JELL–O.
THE IDEA IS TO PUT THE GOOD THINGS IN BEFORE IT SETS!

That was awesome! I've never forgotten that picture. And what a powerful statement in light of how much we now know about early mind development. What a reality check! Say this prayer with me: "Dear God, help me know which good things to put in my child's mind before it sets! Amen."

My sister is an elementary school teacher. For the last thirty years she has worked tirelessly and sacrificially with young children. She is the best example I know of someone who takes advantage of the "window of opportunity." She has one school year to impact, for eternity, the lives in her care. She is underpaid, often underappreciated, and overworked. She doesn't care. She knows her labor is not in vain. A few years ago I cross-stitched these inspirational words from Forest E. Witcraft for her to help spur her on to "love and good deeds" (Hebrews 10:24):

A hundred years from now it will not matter what my bank account was, the sort of house I lived in, or the kind of car I drove, but the world may be different because I was important in the life of a child.[14]

In his book *Raising Your Kids to Love the Lord*, Dave Stone says:

Let's face it. Only perfect parents raise perfect children. (Last time I checked, there were no perfect children and no perfect parents either!) There is no foolproof plan. And there's this little detail called free will, which will determine the spiritual commitment level of your children when they are grown. On the other hand, Christian homes don't just happen; neither do kids who love the Lord. There is a lot we can do to help determine the outcome of our children's spiritual lives. We can become intentional in our efforts. We can pave the way for them. We can model true faith and continually pray that God will transform their hearts. . . . The earlier you begin the process, the better—but it's never too late.[15]

GET SAD, NOT MAD

You know those days when things just happen? Frustrating things, messy things, broken things, disobedience, things that just make you mad? Right? Like every hour? My knee-jerk reaction is anger. Not huge anger, but it isn't pretty. And I am a naturally loud woman, so my outside voice can hurt your ears . . . and your feelings. I do not like this about myself, especially around children. I prayed often about it when my children were toddlers, then preschoolers. I cannot remember who suggested this to me, but I discovered a key. The key that helped lock the door on my loud, ugly anger was to *get sad, not mad.* Something clicked for me and I went into actress mode! If a drink spilled at the table, I would say, "Awww, poor milk. It wanted to be in your tummy, but now it's all over the table and the floor. Let's clean it up." My kids loved it. They would take a paper towel, wipe the milk, and say, "Sorry, milk" and other silly things.

DIS·CI·PLINE:

noun \ \ ˈdi-sə-plən\:

: training that corrects, molds, or perfects the mental faculties or moral character

a : control gained by enforcing obedience or order

b : orderly or prescribed conduct or pattern of behavior

c : self-control[16]

The idea of *sad, not mad* works in disciplining. When children disobey (and they will), you can say, "I'm so sorry you didn't obey. Now I have to discipline you. Next time will you please obey so we can be happy and not sad?" Of course I heard this objection, "No, Mommy, you don't have to if you don't want to." God would help me remember that my highest obedience is to Him, and the Word of God says if we love our children, we will discipline them.

> *Whoever spares the rod hates their children,*
> *but the one who loves their children*
> *is careful to discipline them.*
> PROVERBS 13:24

*For the moment all discipline seems painful rather than
pleasant, but later it yields the peaceful fruit
of righteousness to those who have been trained by it.*

HEBREWS 12:11 [ESV]

*Do not withhold discipline from a child;
even if you strike him with the rod, he will not die.
If you strike him with the rod, you will deliver him
from death. My child, if your heart is wise,
then my heart also will be glad.*

PROVERBS 23:13–15 [NET]

*Folly is bound up in the heart of a child,
but the rod of discipline drives it far from him.*

PROVERBS 22:15 [ESV]

*Fathers, do not provoke your children to anger,
but bring them up in the discipline
and instruction of the Lord.*

EPHESIANS 6:4 [ESV]

*Discipline your son, and he will give you rest;
he will give delight to your heart.*

PROVERBS 29:17 [ESV]

The Bible has given us clear directives about discipline. Our loving Father God disciplines us for our own good, even if we don't feel good in the moment. I liken this discipline to the day I dealt with my son about playing in the street in front of our house. He begged me, then tried tears and bargaining until he realized I would not change my mind. So he gave up. He obeyed and stayed safely in the yard. On that day I, my son, and any neighborhood drivers were spared potential trauma!

Consider the possible outcome of an undisciplined situation. According to Katherine Lee, child expert:

> If you've ever known kids who are not regularly disciplined by their parents, you've probably seen some very stark examples of why it's important to discipline children. Discipline is not only good for children, it is necessary for their happiness and well-being. Discipline is as vital for healthy child development as nutritious food, physical and cognitive. Without discipline, children lack the tools necessary to navigate relationships and challenges in life such as self-discipline, respect for others, and the ability to cooperate with peers.[17]

For me, most of the process of discipline was hard. I heard complaining, fussing, fighting, crying, and it was so frustrating. I hated it! For crying out loud, I'm Miss PattyCake and our life was supposed to be happy and fun all the time! I got tired of constantly hearing, "Why?" I remember thinking, *Please listen to me! I can see what you cannot. I love you and want to keep you safe.*

Do you believe me? Do you know I love you? Do you trust me? If I see danger that you can't see, won't I tell you?

Wait . . . that sounds familiar. I complain to God in the same way. I ask why and fuss and hope God will change my circumstances. Being in this situation with my own child made me very aware of the parental care of Father God. He is my parent and I know He loves me. Will I trust Him the way I ask my children to trust me?

Helen Young speaks of our rare opportunity in this poignant way:

There will be a time when there will be
    no slamming of doors,
      no toys on the stairs, no childhood quarrels,
      no fingerprints on the wallpaper.
Then may I look back with joy and not regret.
God, give me wisdom to see
    that today is my day with my children.
That there is no unimportant moment in their lives.
May I know that no other career is so precious,
    no other work so rewarding,
    no other task so urgent.
May I not defer it nor neglect it,
    but by the Spirit accept it gladly, joyously,
    and by Thy grace realize
That the time is short and my time is now,
For children won't wait.[18]

When my children were little I remember thinking, *Will this mess ever be over?* During that time, my extended family gathered for any and all special occasions with a combined total of ten small children. It really did feel like I was herding cats! Now reading this poem, I am choking back tears because my own children are grown, and I really do miss the "mess." You may want to tape these words to your refrigerator. **Don't miss this rare window of opportunity.**

GIGGLE BREAK

When (not if) one of my children required discipline, I would send the disobedient party to his/her bedroom and give myself a chance to breathe, pray, and let the child think about whatever he or she had done. Then I walked slowly upstairs with the dreaded wooden spoon. One such day I sent my daughter to her room and when I arrived a few minutes later she had done something unexpected. Out of her drawer she had pulled every pair of panties and put them *all on* to pad her little bottom. It was *hilarious*! Pretty creative, if you ask me. I so wish I had taken a picture. She giggled, and I laughed too hard to carry out the punishment. She said sorry, I forgave, we had a "grace" moment and we made a memory.

Chapter 3

ALL-ACCESS PASS

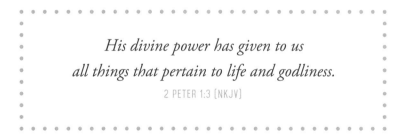

*His divine power has given to us
all things that pertain to life and godliness.*

2 PETER 1:3 [NKJV]

n this verse, did you notice the word "all"? I am pretty sure it means . . . ALL, or everything. I like to think of this verse as the all-access pass to God's provision.

Have you ever had an all-access pass? I remember the first time I went on tour with the Women of Faith conferences, and the staff gave me a laminated badge on a lanyard to hang around my neck. I didn't think much about it until we took a break and went out to lunch. I had to run back to my room for something and was separated from the group, so I went back to the arena alone. All the doors were locked since we were hours from the show, but I finally found a door with a guard. I knocked and he said, "Sorry, this is a restricted area. You can't come in." But I held up my pass and he opened the door and said with a smile, "Welcome." There was power in that pass.

We have God's power in His all-access pass. And the password is *Jesus*.

We have God's power in His all-access pass. And the password is *Jesus*.

WHAT'S MY NAME?

My favorite part of a Miss PattyCake concert event is after the show, when I do a meet-and-greet for families. Dedicated parents stand in line and wait to let their children meet me and hug me and get photos. Over the years I have hugged thousands of little ones and heard some funny things:

- "Miss PattyCake—look! I lost a tooth!"
- "I have a boo-boo."
- "My brother was mean to me."
- "YOU LOOK JUST LIKE MY GRANDMA!" (Really? Hat, gloves, costume? Or am I just that old?)

Sometimes they run to me. Sometimes they are shy. Sometimes they are scared (but not often), and they usually have a story.

This one has stayed with me: A four-year old girl came slowly toward me. I held out my arms to greet her and said, "Hi there! What is your beautiful name?" She looked at me wide-eyed and said, "Uh . . . UH . . . UH. . . ." She turned away and screamed, "MOMMY, WHAT'S MY NAME?!"

Do you ever feel that way? So overwhelmed you can hardly remember your own name? Caring for and parenting little ones can be exhausting and terrifying. I don't know about you, but I clearly remember a day I said to myself, *What was I thinking? I just wanted a baby, but I got a **person**! And now I am the one responsible for this person!*

KITCHEN HELP

I remember this day in my kitchen: Christopher was probably ten months old and in the high chair, crying. Marilyn was two and on the floor, loudly banging a wooden spoon on a pan I had given her. She was singing and making "music." Usually I encourage this and sing along, but this morning I had HAD IT. The kitchen was a mess—the baby had thrown his food on the floor, and I felt like crying, too. I hit the wall and did the only thing I knew to do . . . I yelled, "Lord Jesus!" Well, that shut the kids up. They both were scared, I think. Wide-eyed, they looked at their mommy.

That didn't stop me. I closed my eyes and kept yelling, "HELP ME! I do not know how to do this!" You should know I was thirty-four years old before I became a parent. I had been a professional singer, teacher, church staff member, and worship leader, and I had traveled around the world. All of that was easy compared to this new job. Now my husband was at work with our only car. I was stuck in a rental house in a new city where I knew very few people, and I was alone with these children.

The baby cried more. My two-year-old thought my yelling was a new song or game and she joined me! She shouted with me in her little voice, "Lord Jesus, help Mommy!" That was grace to me. I felt the nudge—the quiet thought came to my mind, *You are trying too hard. Stop, enjoy the moment, take a break.* I took a deep breath, scooped my boy from the high chair, and put him on the floor with me. I gave him a spoon, and the three of us made a racket, banging on pots, making a "joyful noise" (Psalm 100:1 KJV). I was crying and laughing, the kids were having fun and eating Cheerios off the floor. And it didn't bother me one bit. And there was joy in the journey. My friend Sheila Walsh says, "Jesus lives close to the floor." After all, Jesus's other name is Emmanuel, which means "God with us" (Matthew 1:23).

Not long after that day I was reading my Bible and saw this verse: "Call out for insight and cry aloud for understanding"

(Proverbs 2:3). Next to that verse in my Bible I wrote, "I did that!" And I had a good laugh. I always think of God watching us the way we watch our children, smiling and laughing at the things we do, occasionally elbowing an angel and saying, "Did you see that?!"

The story about the little girl who forgot her name has an ending. When she turned to her mommy and asked, "What's my name?" her mother calmly said, "Your name is Rebekah, and I am here with you." That spoke volumes to me. We all need reminding that we have a parent—Father God—who knows our names and is here with us.

We need to hear from God as we care for the children in our lives. We NEED His wisdom.

Also He knows what we need. Here again is the promise: "His divine power has given to us all things that pertain to life and godliness" (2 Peter 1:3 NKJV). Did you catch the words "all things"? The NIV translation reads, "His divine power has given us everything we need for a godly life." Jesus said, "Your Father knows what you need before you ask him" (Matthew 6:8). We need to hear from God as we care for the children in our lives. We NEED His wisdom.

Solomon is considered one of the wisest men who ever lived. He authored several parts of the Bible, and much is written of his life. In 1 Kings 3:5–10, the Lord appeared to him and said, "Ask for whatever you want me to give you." Solomon asked for an understanding mind and a "discerning heart" to govern the people and "distinguish between right and wrong." In Hebrew, the word *understanding* is defined as "a hearing ear."[1]

God gives wisdom, knowledge, and understanding (hearing ears) to those who ask.

WHEN I THINK ABOUT THE HELP I NEED,
I REMEMBER GOD TOLD SOLOMON TO ASK.

ASK

We have access to everything we need:

*God will meet all your needs according
to the riches of his glory in Christ Jesus.*

PHILIPPIANS 4:19

. . . .

*"Ask and it will be given to you; seek and you will find;
knock and the door will be opened to you."*

MATTHEW 7:7

. . . .

*Praise be to the God and Father of our Lord Jesus Christ,
who has blessed us in the heavenly realms
with every spiritual blessing in Christ.*

EPHESIANS 1:3

. . . .

*"Call to me and I will answer you and tell you great
and unsearchable things you do not know."*
JEREMIAH 33:3

Those are just a very few examples of God's promise to help us. And just look at this:

"I the LORD have spoken, and I will do it."
EZEKIEL 36:36

Woohoo! YAY, GOD! As my grandfather would say, "You can hang your hat on that!" And just in case you think it is up to you to figure everything out, work harder, be better, remember this huge truth:

*It is God who works in you both to will
and to do for His good pleasure.*
PHILIPPIANS 2:13 (NKJV)

So it is God . . . working *in* me and *through* me. That's good news because He is a lot smarter than I am. Here's a question: Is caring for, loving, teaching, and protecting children part of "His good pleasure"? The answer is, as my children would say, "DUH." Jesus said, "Let the little children come to me, and do not hinder them, for the kingdom of heaven belongs to such as these" (Matthew 19:14). When you and I participate in the spiritual formation of these little ones, we are taking part in kingdom work. I hope that makes you smile.

Have I not commanded you?
Be strong and courageous.
Do not be afraid; do not be discouraged,
for the LORD your God
will be with your wherever you go.

JOSHUA 1:9

This verse was on my mirror for years. And when I thought about being "strong and courageous," I remembered God could do strong and courageous work in me and through me. I just need to ask!

WE HAVE ACCESS TO MORE THAN WE KNOW

My pastor, Scotty Smith at Christ Community Church in Franklin, Tennessee, told this story during a sermon. I have never forgotten it:

There was a man who saved and saved for a cruise. He had dreamed for years of traveling on a ship, and he used almost every dime he had to buy the ticket. He was having a wonderful time and enjoying all the sights, but his chair was empty at every meal. Finally, one of the stewards went to his cabin and said, "We have noticed you missed your meals with us for the past few days. Is anything wrong? Can we change the menu for you or get you something special to eat?"

"Oh, NO," the man replied. "I only had enough money to pay for my room, and I just can't afford the meals, so I brought along some crackers and cheese, and other snacks. Don't worry about me."

Taken aback, the steward said, "Did no one tell you? All your meals are included in the ticket price. All the food is available to you—at no extra cost. There is a buffet with all you can eat!"

"Buffet? BUFFET! NO WAY!"[2]

That's right, ladies and gentleman—the cruise includes all the food you can eat, available 24/7! What a fabulous picture of the abundant life God wants to give all of us who have put our hope in the Lord Jesus. We have safe passage to an eternal home with Him in heaven, we have a passport to that new country, we have this world in all its beauty to enjoy as we travel, and that feels like abundant life to me. If that idea of abundance is not enough to wrap your brain around, consider this: the Bible says God will give even more!

> *[God] is able to do exceedingly abundantly*
> *above all that we ask or think.*
> EPHESIANS 3:20 (NKJV)

If your child is anything like mine, and most other children, you are being *asked* questions all day, every day, until you want to cover your ears and scream!

Mommy, can I have _____?
Can I go _____?
Can I do _____?

Can I watch _____?
Can I play _____?
Can I eat _____?
Can I drink _____?
What is this?
How much can I have?
How high is the sky?
How do birds fly?
Why can't I _____?

Do any of these sound familiar? No? That means your child can't talk yet! A friend of mine gave me a little sign that says, "Raising children is like being pecked to death by a chicken." RIGHT? We are doing the best we can to answer each request, be fair and honest, be kind, give what we feel is appropriate and wise, and do the right thing as a parent/caregiver. Where do we think these ideas originated? We are made in His image; our instincts are God-breathed. Jesus talked about this very thing one day to a large crowd. He said, "Which of you, if your son asks for bread, will give him a stone? Or if he asks for a fish, will give him a snake? If you, then, though you are evil, know how to give good gifts to your children, how much more will your Father in heaven give good gifts to those who ask him!" (Matthew 7:9–11).

I remember that verse as my 7-Eleven verse. When I was growing up there weren't many quick-stop stores, the only one was 7-Eleven (so named for its hours of operation). This is a quick-stop verse. If we need something, we can ask—and believe, because . . .

This is the confidence we have in approaching God:
that if we ask anything according to his will,
he hears us. And if we know that
he hears us—whatever we ask—
we know that we have what we asked of him.

1 JOHN 5:14–15

Miss PattyCake even has hand motions for this idea that you can share with your children. Put your hand out, palm up, and say, "Ask!" (Go on, do it.) Now, make a fist and put it to your chest. Say, "Believe!"

• •

So, what do you think? With God on our side like this,
how can we lose? If God didn't hesitate to put everything
on the line for us, embracing our condition
and exposing himself to the worst by sending his own Son,
is there anything else he wouldn't gladly
and freely do for us?

ROMANS 8:31–32 (MSG)

• •

I recently heard a pastor say, "When we are in Christ we are given a first-class ticket, but we insist on traveling in coach."

Who wouldn't want to travel first-class? I'm not suggesting our lives should be cozy, always cushy, with all the food and drink we want. Jesus said, "In the world you'll have trouble. But cheer up! I have overcome the world" (John 16:33 GW). Since the same Spirit who raised Jesus from the dead lives in us (Romans

8:11), we have access to the overcoming power that produces joy in us for the journey through this life. Joy is a gift of God. I am not talking about just a good feeling we should be having all day in the middle of diapers, baby food, toys on the floor, dishes in the sink, laundry, cooking, working, and more. We cannot possibly manufacture in ourselves a sense of joy during those moments.

I remember so many mornings at five thirty—almost on the dot—our little boy would stand by my bed and shake my shoulder, shouting, "MOMMY, GET UP, GET UP!" *Ugh*. I am not a morning person. And I did not feel cheerful. I prayed for a smile before opening my eyes and tried to answer the little guy nicely. But honestly, I wanted to knock him out! I mean, not really, but just sort of encourage him to go back to sleep for thirty more minutes. I can't be cheerful by myself—I need help. And we've seen that help comes from above.

COLORFUL ACCESS

I'm a visual learner. I love pictures and I love color. I especially love color pictures. You should see my house. My children say I'm a color junkie!

I imagine this picture when I need help—and I know where my help comes from! I see the Father with His hand on a big lever connected to a bright-pink fire hose. Let's say I am having a hard time being nice to someone and I'm about to lose control to anger. I close my eyes and breathe (it's very important to breathe before you speak) and see God calmly walk to the hose labeled Kindness. He waits for me to ask, then He flips that lever and *whoosh*, kindness pours through the hose and right into me. Like a pipe, kindness runs through me and spills out onto that nasty someone (who is often my own child).

Have you ever wondered how can such small people can bring out the worst in us? My mother used to say, "No one can bring something out of you that is not already there." I hated hearing that. But it is true, and it reminds me of my need for help.

Moments like that are an opportunity for God to remind us of the all-access pass we have through Him. Whatever we need, anytime, all the time: Jesus said, "I will talk to the Father, and he'll provide you another Friend so that you will always have someone with you. This Friend is the Spirit of Truth. . . . You know him already because he has been staying with you, and will even be *in* you!" (John 14:16–17 MSG). This Friend is the Holy Spirit! He is equipping us and changing us so we look and act more like Jesus. And if you have read much about Jesus, He was a pretty "colorful" person!

Wouldn't you like some color—some flavor in your daily life? How about something like a big, red apple; a juicy, green pear; a bright-yellow banana; or a delicious orange? I like to think of God's help in terms of the fruit of the Holy Spirit. This fruit is given to all who believe and have received Jesus. The fruit is *in us* because the Holy Spirit (the Friend) is *in us*.

But the fruit of the Spirit is love, joy, peace, patience,
kindness, goodness, faithfulness, gentleness, self control;
against such things there is no law.

GALATIANS 5:22–23 (ESV)

Did you notice the word "fruit" is singular? There is one fruit with many *flavors*—or as I like to think, many *colors*.

Here is your **all-access color pass** to the fruit of the Spirit:

LOVE	white (pure, clean)
JOY	yellow (sunny, happy)
PEACE	green (a fresh, grassy meadow)
PATIENCE	blue (an ocean, the sky, wide and big)
KINDNESS	gold (great worth, makes you rich to give or receive)
GOODNESS	orange (juicy, healthy, life-giving vitamin C)
FAITHFULNESS	red (blood brothers who stick together)
GENTLENESS	pink (a newborn baby)
SELF-CONTROL	purple (royal color—the king of the fruit)

This works for me as a visual learner. Does it help you?

As I write this, I am sitting at my kitchen table looking at a fabulous, wildly colorful painting of a royal crown. My friend Ginnie Johnson is the artist. When I first saw this painting, it nearly took my breath away. Ginnie travels all over, telling women we are the King's daughters (www.kings-daughters.com). Her work is always signed with the verse, "The King's daughter is all glorious within" (Psalm 45:13 NASB). God is coloring our world by His Spirit with all His fruit! Let God color you and you will become all glorious within.

I once heard this story: A mommy was busy working in her kitchen while her little girl was playing, singing, doing her three-year-old thing. Soon the mommy realized it had gotten quiet. *Uh-oh.* Nervously she went to check. She found her darling girl in the bathroom standing by the sink, smearing red lipstick all over her face. Before the mother could even speak, her daughter said, "Look, Mommy, I painted you all over me!"

God wants to paint Himself all over us. He wants to change us into the image of His dear Son, the One who loves us and gave Himself for us. Jesus came to give us life abundant, a colorful, joyful life. And He will use the children in our world to speed the process along. It is interesting the way we see our own strengths and weaknesses when our buttons are pushed. Who can push those buttons more than our children? And they may not even be teenagers yet! Like the proverbial squeezing that produces juice, we see what is really inside us.

I had always considered myself a pretty happy, easygoing woman until my children revealed in me some "color" I did not like. Have you seen that in your life? Holy Spirit to the rescue! He reminded me I have *access* to the colorful fruit of God inside me. For me it is like being in a dark house and forgetting there is electricity. Asking for God's help turns on the lights! Voilà! You *can* act and live **fruitfully and colorfully**.

A SCARY CAT DAY

It was nearly noon and the trip to the grocery store had taken longer than I wanted. All three of us were cranky. Grocery shopping takes more energy than I ever think it will, and it really wears out the children. I finally checked out, wrestled them into the car, and drove toward home.

"Mommy, I'm hungry. I'm thirsty, too. How long till we get home? Will it rain today? What color is the moon? Do fish have teeth? Christopher won't be quiet!" (Do the questions ever end?!)

Even getting out of the car was a chore. My ten-month-old son was fussing loudly and was heavy on my right arm in the car seat while my other arm was loaded with grocery bags. "Go straight into the house, please," I instructed two-year-old Marilyn, who slowly walked up the front porch stairs in front of me. I felt like a shepherd, herding her toward the door. Time for lunch and naps. "Please hurry! Mommy is TIRED."

She suddenly stopped, screamed, and ran to the other end of our wide front porch. There was a kitty near our front door. Not our kitty—a strange kitty—a big, hairy cat. She was terrified! Speaking soothing words to Marilyn, I walked calmly past the cat to the door. It looked at me. I looked

> God wants to paint Himself all over us. He wants to change us into the image of His dear Son, the One who loves us and gave Himself for us.

at it. It didn't move. I unlocked the front door, being careful not to drop bags or baby. "Come on, sweetie. Mommy sees the cat. The cat won't get you." I shooed the cat. It lazily walked a few feet from the door. Marilyn was not moving. "Honey, I won't let the cat hurt you."

"The cat, THE CAT!" she wailed.

Holding the door open I said, "The kitty will not hurt you. Just please run on into the house."

"No, NO, it's a BIG CAT," she whined.

Frustrated, I said, "Marilyn, look at me. Don't look at the cat. Walk to me and come in the house." She didn't move. My arms were aching now. "Please, honey—don't look at the cat. I will not let the cat hurt you. Look at me." I was begging, rather loudly now. The baby was crying, and I was on the brink. "Sweetie! If that cat comes anywhere near you, I will scare it away!"

Finally, after much coaxing, Marilyn took a tentative step, looked at me, then the cat, then me, then the cat, then me, and ran past me into the house. WHEW! I turned to the cat, stomped my foot, and said, "SCAT!" The strange cat flew off our porch. We never saw it again.

I have found mothering to be the place where I learn the most about God's fathering.

Later I pondered that episode and had an *aha moment*. (I hope you have those occasionally, too.) How like our Father to show me something profound in a typical mothering day. A silly cat moment became this lesson: I am that scared little girl—afraid of the "cats" in my life. The Father says, "Look at Me—not the cats. Keep your eyes on Me—I will not let the 'cats' hurt you. Walk the way I show you. I am a good Shepherd, herding you to a safe place. I have set before you an open door. Trust Me. Rely on Me."

I have found mothering to be the place where I learn the most about God's fathering. Today, ask the Father to show you how your parenting can reflect His parenting. He's able to SCAT THE CAT!

. . . .

You keep him in perfect peace whose mind is stayed on you, because he trusts in you.

ISAIAH 26:3 (ESV)

. . . .

MASTER KEY

The icon I used for this chapter is a key. The master key giving us access to God's "all" is **prayer**.

Pray? How do we do that? Does it sound complicated? Intimidating? Some of us have this idea that prayer can only happen when we are alone, quiet, maybe on our knees, early in the morning, or at the end of the day. When you have babies and little children those opportunities are rare, so this thinking might lead you to believe you can't use the master key. We have been talking about asking and have seen many scriptures inviting us, encouraging us to ask. This, of course, is prayer but only one type.

What if prayer is different from what you think? What if prayer can simply be a thought you turn toward the Father at any time? What if you don't even need words? As you know, the children in your care don't always use words to communicate. You know the "I'm hungry" cry and the "I'm angry" or "I'm happy" noises. Sometimes in the routine of caring for children, we don't have words either, and that is okay. Look at this: "The

Spirit helps us in our weakness. We do not know what we ought to pray for, but the Spirit himself intercedes for us through wordless groans" (Romans 8:26).

Prayer can happen all day, every day, all the time, anytime. It's easy to chat with someone who knows you well. And who knows you better than anyone? God, the One who made you. God, the One who loves you. Prayer is an ongoing conversation with the One who loves you, and He is always listening.

Max Lucado has written a book called *Before Amen.* In it, after studying prayers all through the Bible, he sums up the essence of a petition in a simple way. Here is Max's "pocket prayer": "Father, you are good. I need help. They need help. Thank you. In Jesus' name, Amen."[3]

So let's recap:

. . . .

God knows our names!
God knows what we need!
He wants to give us what we need!
We have an **all-access pass** *through Jesus!*
We have access to more than we know.
God's colorful fruit is ours, and He wants to "paint" us
to look like Himself!
We have the master key of prayer.
Remember to **ask.**
God is a good parent and loves to **give** *to His children!*

. . . .

GIGGLE BREAK

When our son was almost four, he had a terrible asthma episode and had to be rushed to the emergency room. His heartbeat was accelerated and he didn't respond well to the medicine, so he had to stay overnight. I sat by his bed with my hand on him, praying. Thinking he was asleep, I was praying out loud for quite a while until he rolled over and said, "Mommy, who are you talking to?"

Reese (age three) learning the Lord's Prayer:
"Our Father, who does art in heaven,
Harold is His name. . . . Lead us not into temptation,
deliver us from e-mail."

My cousin Alan (age three) was asked to pray
at the Thanksgiving dinner.
Fifteen or more heads bowed around the table
and my aunt Jane was so proud as they
waited for him to begin.
Awkward silence.
Then he quietly asked,
"Mommy, what's that man's name?"

Chapter 4

INFANCY

Oh yes, you shaped me first inside, then out; you formed me
in my mother's womb. I thank you, High God—
you're breathtaking! Body and soul, I am marvelously made!
I worship in adoration—what a creation!
You know me inside and out, you know every bone in
my body; you know exactly how I was made, bit by bit,
how I was sculpted from nothing into something.
Like an open book, you watched me grow
from conception to birth; all the stages of my life
were spread out before you, the days of my life
all prepared before I'd even lived one day.

PSALM 139:13–16 [MSG]

t's a . . . *GIRL*! My husband and I decided there were too few surprises in life, so we waited until the birth for the big news. She had blue eyes and blond hair! Another surprise, since we both have brown eyes and hair. And what a voice—that baby could cry! "Just like her mother," my husband said (not the crying, the volume). Her birth was an emotional high point in my life. "For this child I prayed, and the Lord has granted me my petition that I made to him," said Hannah in 1 Samuel 1:27 (ESV). I, like Hannah, had prayed for a baby.

I just wanted a *baby*—I mean, my friends had babies, I was already past thirty, and my parents wanted grandchildren, so I asked God for a baby. What God gave me instead was a *person*! So then I had this little person in my arms. And this was not Costco—I could not take her back. Pretty scary if you think about it, right?

So—how to begin? She didn't come with a manual, for crying out loud! How could I begin this journey of parenting?

THE IMPORTANCE OF NOW

We mommies think these days will never end: the diapers, the messy bottoms, feeding and feeding and not sleeping, the crying, the wondering, *Is she okay?* the runny nose, changing her clothes, in the car seat, out of the car seat, trips to the doctor, awake, asleep, do it all again tomorrow. The wise Erma Bombeck said this about motherhood:

We go about our daily routine, stringing one brightly colored wooden bead after another, feeling pretty proud of ourselves. We assume we're accomplishing so much, but the illusion of productivity is shattered when, at the end of the day, we look down at our necklace only to discover that there is no knot. The once-strung beads are now scattered all over the place, and we have to start all over.[1]

This thought is echoed in *What Every Mom Needs* by Elisa Morgan and Carol Kuykendall:

When do moms get to finish anything? We can't finish a meal without getting up and running to the stove, or the refrigerator, or to answer the phone. We scarcely finish a thought before somebody needs something and we've lost our concentration. The very job of mothering (caregiving) is unending.[2]

In those early days I slept little, read all the books I had, called my mom every day, listened to all the advice anyone gave, and it seemed every hour brought a discovery—velvet-soft skin, perfect hand curled around my finger, tiny sharp fingernails, listening for any sound, nursing her, dressing her, changing her, watching her little face in wonder, amazed by her breathing and tiny heartbeat. It was fascinating and terrifying at the same time. What if I dropped and broke her? What if I ate something that made her sick? What if I slept through a feeding? What if—? Can you guess what my one-word prayer was? Say it with me: "HELP!"

The day came to take her for those dreaded shots. I remember it well. I carefully got her into the car seat and drove like a snail to the doctor. It was traumatic . . . for me. That perfect trusting face was looking around peacefully until she felt the needle, then this slow-motion transformation as she realized she felt pain. She cried. I cried. It was awful. The nurse looked at my tears, patted my knee, and said, "Don't worry, honey. The mommies always cry more than the babies."

Very late that night I was awake nursing and changing her. When I rolled her over I accidentally touched that spot on her hip that was tender from the vaccination. Out came her loud cry! I was devastated. I didn't mean to hurt her. She cried, I cried again and then began talking to her (as if she could understand me): "I'm sorry! Oh, sweet baby, I am so very sorry you are in pain. I didn't want to hurt you, but you needed those shots and they are good for you and you will never be sick with those diseases and believe me, if there was any other way. . . ." I kept talking until she calmed down and I stopped crying. And then—a moment when God helped me. An obscure verse popped into my head:

"I am going to do something in your days that you would not believe, even if you were told."

HABAKKUK 1:5

There I was weeping over my child's pain, trying to explain it to her, knowing she could not understand my words, and God had said the same thing. He was about to do something that I could not understand or believe, even if He told me.

That night I got something new—something MORE. The verse in Habakkuk was, to me, a revelation of God's watchful care, and I got it—He sees me, knows my pain, and wants me to trust His kind intention even when I don't understand. That was a page-turning day for me. I knew God loved me and wanted me to know Him, but there was something more—I now knew a mother's love, which had ushered me into a new depth of knowing the Father. I knew it was my job to teach this little person about God—the Father—and the time to start was now, before she could even understand.

This is not a new idea:

> You know that the beginning is the most important
> part of any work, especially in the case
> of a young and tender thing;
> for that is the time at which the character
> is being formed and the desired
> impression is more readily taken.
>
> PLATO, 380 BC[3]

We humans instinctively know that if we do not care for living things in the beginning, they will probably not survive.

. . . .

I knew God loved me and wanted me to know Him, but there was something more— I now knew a mother's love, which had ushered me into a new depth of knowing the Father.

. . . .

Of course you know this as a parent, grandparent, or caregiver when it pertains to basic needs of life, but it is true in *all* developmental areas, especially spiritual. Child expert and author Jeanne Hendricks said:

> To the newborn child, people are everything. The earliest social skill is when that little infant can find and hold the eyes of an adult in what we call the "quiet-alert" stage. . . . It's when that little one looks at you and says, "Can I trust you?" Because the first developmental task of a newborn child is to find out, "Is this a safe world? Am I going to be accepted and loved?"[4]

Most parents and caregivers think about these things:

- Mother's milk, formula, or combination?
- Should I use a pacifier?
- Do I have the right colors in her room for mental stimulation?
- Am I talking enough/too much to her?
- How should I exercise those little arms and legs?
- Do I have the right music for helping synapses connect?
- What will help her stop crying?
- Does she have an allergy?
- Is she mentally and emotionally normal?

Have you driven yourself, and others, crazy talking, researching, and trying to get it all right? Probably.

As important as a baby's diet and exercise are for physical, mental, and emotional development and stimulation, who is talking to you about your child's spiritual development?

SPIRITUAL FORMATION

What is spiritual formation? It is the foundation upon which salvation and faith are built. This verse showed me where to lay the first bricks in that foundation:

> From infancy *you have known the Holy Scriptures,*
> *which are able to make you wise for salvation*
> *through faith in Christ Jesus.*
> 2 TIMOTHY 3:15 [EMPHASIS MINE]

Here is what I like about this verse: it references the life of baby Timothy. Seldom in the Bible are we given the names of caregivers, but with Timothy, we know who they were: his mother and grandmother, Eunice and Lois. Both of these women took the time and made the effort to sing, speak, and teach little Timothy the Word of God.

The story of Lois and Eunice should encourage all mothers who are striving to raise their children to know God. Working as a team, Lois and Eunice used their strong faith and knowledge of scripture to raise Timothy to be the strong Christian leader he was. The commitment to maintaining a Christian household is what allowed Timothy to become one of Paul's most trusted friends and disciples. Paul writes of Lois and Eunice in 2 Timothy 1:5, saying, "I am reminded of your sincere faith, which first lived in your grandmother Lois and in your mother Eunice and, I am persuaded, now lives in you also."

Timothy's faith proves the value of being raised in a Christian home. Through the Christian atmosphere Lois and Eunice created, these two women influenced Timothy's faith, training him to know and love the Lord. These strong, godly women exemplified the Christian lifestyle, creating a household that shaped Timothy's faith and inspires our own. Their unwavering faith and commitment to sharing God's Word and demonstrating His love illustrates how strong women of faith should raise up their children and households.[5]

Bestselling author of *The Seven Habits of Highly Effective People*, Stephen Covey, has wisely said, "begin with the end in mind."[6] What is the end? I hope you, like Lois and Eunice, want the end to be a vital, authentic relationship with God the Father through Jesus, empowered by the Holy Spirit. That is what starting early can do. When we pour into little lives the love of God and the Word of God, we are preparing them for salvation that comes only through Christ.

• •

Stick with what you learned and believed,
sure of the integrity of your teachers—why, you took in
the sacred Scriptures with your mother's milk!
There's nothing like the written Word of God for showing
you the way to salvation through faith in Christ Jesus.

2 TIMOTHY 3:14–15 [MSG]

• •

God has given to us parents, grandparents, caregivers, and teachers the role of influencer in little lives. We don't always think that what we are saying and doing is working inside the spirit and soul of a little person . . . but it is! And it will become like a concrete foundation.

GET STARTED EARLY!

Billy Graham said, "The greatest surprise in life to me is the brevity of life."[7]

Even when you think these early years are going on and on and wonder, *When will this child ever be potty trained?* remember this: Looking back, you will be surprised how quickly your little one has grown.

Don't think spiritual formation is someone else's job. Don't think, *I take them to church, what more can I do?* Even if they cannot understand your words, they do soak in life—because "the word of God is alive and active" (Hebrews 4:12).

I have discovered, especially working with special-needs children, that even when all the synapses don't connect correctly and the children don't always understand our words, they absorb a deeper understanding and knowing. There is a planting of life that happens when we speak and sing the living Word of God to our babies!

Do you wonder, as I did, if all the effort we are making in the early months and years really matters? Will they remember the songs, the activities, the stories? It is an understandable concern. What we do know is this: Without a firm foundation, a structure cannot stand. The foundation is underground and often unseen. But without it, a structure falls. Jesus told the story of a house built on sand and compared that to a house built on a rock (see Matthew 7:24–27). Which house stood? What you are helping develop in little lives is a foundation on which they can stand. Your labor is not in vain.

> *"It is the same with my word. I send it out, and it always produces fruit. It will accomplish all I want it to."*
> ISAIAH 55:11 [NLT]

Here's the same verse in *The Message* translation:

> *"So will the words that come out of my mouth not come back empty-handed. They'll do the work I sent them to do, they'll complete the assignment I gave them."*
> ISAIAH 55:11 [MSG]

Infants are sponges. They soak up whatever touches them. Give them plenty of "washing with water through the word" (Ephesians 5:26). It is living water and will nourish their spirits. You can trust God to use what you invest in little lives.

> Proverbs 22:6 says,
> *Start children off on the way they should go,*
> *and even when they are old they will not turn from it.*

. . . .

> *Point your kids in the right direction—*
> *when they're old they won't be lost.*
> PROVERBS 22:6 [MSG]

GIGGLE BREAK

A three-year old raptly watched his mother nurse his new baby sister. As he looked on, he innocently asked, "What comes out of those nozzles?" Smiling, his mother said, "It's milk." He then asked, "Is one hot and one cold, or is one white and one chocolate?"

Chapter 5

SEVEN WAYS TO PRACTICE PRAISE

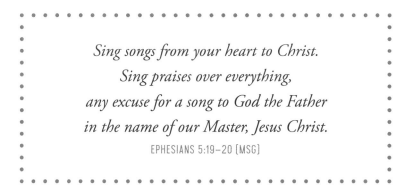

Sing songs from your heart to Christ.
Sing praises over everything,
any excuse for a song to God the Father
in the name of our Master, Jesus Christ.
EPHESIANS 5:19–20 [MSG]

Let's begin with this truth: When we turn our attention to God and give Him thanks and praise, it changes us. When we tell Him who **He** is, He reminds us who **we** are. We are His children, heirs to all the promises. He empowers us—and let's face it, we all need help!

Early in my life I discovered the power of praise. This is how it began for me: I was a college student studying music as a vocal performance major. I loved opera, musical theater, and show choir. I dreamed of singing in New York or on a cruise ship, or just anywhere on a stage.

Enter Jesus. He took center stage in my life and began to change me. His words encouraged me: "Sing, sing your hearts out to God!" (Colossians 3:16 MSG).

And the big one for me:

He put a new song in my mouth,
a song of praise *to our God.*
PSALM 40:3 [ESV, EMPHASIS MINE]

At that time I wasn't completely sure what all those verses meant. Sure, I had sung plenty of hymns and classical music with the words, "Praise God." But just what was this "new song" God was telling me to sing? That question launched my journey toward what God wanted to do with the music He had given me.

PRAISE IS THE PATHWAY INTO HIS PRESENCE.

Psalm 100:4 says,

> *Enter his gates with thanksgiving*
> *and his courts with praise;*
> *give thanks to him and praise his name.*

A quick look at the layout of the temple or the tabernacle in the time of King David shows us this geography or floor plan. You had to walk through the gates of the temple to get into the area where sacrifice and cleansing took place. To come into the place of God's presence, where He is by His Spirit, we must enter His courts. The Bible explains that before Jesus, only the priests were allowed to enter the courts. But now, because of Jesus's life, death, and resurrection, we are all priests and can enter His courts with praise. 1 Peter 2:4-5 confirms this: "As you come to him, the living Stone—rejected by humans but chosen by God and precious to him—you also, like living stones, are being built into a spiritual house to be a holy priesthood, offering spiritual sacrifices acceptable to God through Jesus Christ."

Because of this revelation, I began to sing praises to God and I was changed! Truly it is "good to give thanks to the LORD, and to *sing praises*" (Psalm 92:1 NKJV, emphasis mine). Not only that—there is more. Isaiah 61:3 (AMP) says God will give us "the garment [expressive] of praise instead of a disheartened spirit." That is good news! This truth changed my life then and still energizes me today! This energy is something we all need, especially as we parent and care for little ones.

As followers of Jesus, we need to know *who* we are, *what* we are to do, and *how* to live in the presence of God because "times of refreshing may come from the Lord" (Acts 3:19). The Bible says, "Thou art holy, O thou that inhabitest [lives in] the praises of Israel" (Psalm 22:3 KJV). The Hebrew word used for "praises" in this verse means "to sing."[1] The New International Version uses the word "enthroned" instead of "inhabitest." When we sing praises, God is enthroned. I have been in a service where they actually placed a chair in the middle of the stage to represent the place God inhabits when we sing.

Sing? Wow—what a concept! As Miss PattyCake, I love to encourage parents and caregivers to . . .

SING YOUR WAY THROUGH YOUR DAY!

There are other ways to give God praise, and we will look at those, but this is so important to know: Music is "magic." It is the fastest, most permanent way to get information into our minds. Music works! Much of our educational system uses music as a memorization tool. Throughout the early childhood and elementary years, music has proved to be the medium of choice for effective learning. The ancient world knew only the oral traditions. Every culture passed down its stories, traditions, laws, and heritage through music. We know that all young Jews were required to learn the Law of Moses, the prophets, the Psalms and Proverbs, and all of it was set to music.[2] As a parent and teacher I have effectively used music to teach about God's great big world, God's character, Bible stories, and educational fundamentals. Music can easily create an atmosphere and language for giving God thanks and praise in an age-appropriate way. Before I get too excited about the *how-to* part of praising God, let's begin with the *what*.

WHAT IS PRAISE?

That was my question when I felt urged by God to embrace the verse I mentioned earlier: "He put a new song in my mouth, a hymn of praise to our God" (Psalm 40:3). *The Message* puts it this way: "He taught me how to sing the latest God-song, a praise-song to our God." Over the years I have done a lot of reading and studying about praise, and this summary by a seminary professor, Dr. Bruce Leafblad, is my favorite: "PRAISE is celebrative worship in which believers magnify and exalt the Lord through expressive acts, enthusiastically proclaiming the unrivaled excellence of His Name, His character, and His actions in a spirit of *uninhibited rejoicing!*"[3]

The energy and language of Dr. Leafblad's summary fits my personality! It is exciting to know God loves celebrations and loves our rejoicing. As a mommy I am always looking for a way to celebrate with my children, and if they rejoice *with* me it is even better. I researched the word *praise* in many places for a more encompassing picture of exactly what God is asking of us. Check out the *Illustrated Bible Dictionary* definition:

> The praise of man toward God is the means by which we express our joy to the Lord. We are commanded to praise God both for who He is and for what He does (Psalm150:2). Praising God for who He is is called adoration; praising Him for what he does is known as thanksgiving. Praise of God may be in song or prayer, individually or collectively, spontaneous or prearranged; originating from the emotions or from the will.[4]

WHAT IS WORSHIP?

These days we hear a lot about worship. We go to *worship* service. We sing praise and *worship* songs. Since praise is always biblically defined as something we do, what is *worship*? This calls for definition and clarification.

The word *worship* has Anglo-Saxon roots and comes from "worth-ship," which speaks of the value placed on someone or something.[5] When we value someone, we demonstrate it with gifts, time, and/or thanks. Translated from the Greek word *proskyneo*, worship means, "to come near and kiss (the hand), denotes reverence and humility, to prostrate oneself before."[6]

I also looked for a good definition of what the Bible terms "worship." Graham Kendrick offers this:

WORSHIP is the whole of life. It's not that we fit worship into our lives, but we fit our lives into worship. Worship is the process of getting nearer to our God. If we think that worship is just a time of singing, we have missed it. Worship is the overflow of our ever-deepening relationship with God, and that embraces the whole of life, not just a couple of hours on a Sunday.[7]

When we worship (value, honor, come near to God), we will sense God's enjoyment of us and our enjoyment of Him. "For the LORD takes delight in his people; he crowns the humble with victory" (Psalm 149:4).

The Westminster Shorter Catechism asks these questions:

Q. What is the chief end of man?
A. Man's chief end is to glorify God, and to enjoy him forever.

Q. What rule hath God given to direct us how we may glorify and enjoy him?
A. The Word of God, which is contained in the Scriptures of the Old and New Testaments, is the only rule to direct us how we may glorify and enjoy him.[8]

GLORIFY + ENJOY = WORSHIP!

Since worship is our goal, our purpose, our destiny—how do we worship? Psalm 100:4 is the simplest instruction I know: "Enter his gates with thanksgiving and his courts with praise."

Praise is a decision. Praise can also be a verb. It is something we *do*. Praise escorts us into His presence, where we worship, know, and enjoy Him. I love this quote:

• •

Praise is the golden bridge
to the heart of God.

CATHERINE MARSHALL[9]

• •

WHY PRAISE?

1. We are created for praise.
   (Isaiah 43:21; Ephesians 1:13–14)
2. We are commanded to praise.
   (Psalm 113:1, Psalm 150)
3. We are called to praise.
   (1 Peter 2:9)

Before we are called to be preachers, teachers, missionaries, or parents, grandparents, or caregivers, we are called to worship as priests. 1 Peter 2:9 tells us: "You are a chosen people, a royal priesthood, a holy nation, God's special possession, that you may declare the praises of him who called you out of darkness into his wonderful light!"

REASONS FOR PRAISE

- God inhabits (lives in) it. (Psalm 22:3 KJV)
- God speaks to us. (Psalm 68:32–33, Psalm 25:14)
- Praise refines us. (Proverbs 27:21)
- It glorifies God. (Psalm 50:23)
- It generates power. (Psalm 84, Psalm 149, Psalm 8:2)
- It precedes victory. (2 Chronicles 20)
- It is the purpose of God's people. (Isaiah 43:21)

Are you convinced yet? Are you thinking, *Wow, this sounds pretty powerful?* Psalm 107:8 (KJV) states: "Oh that men would *praise* the LORD" (emphasis mine). Praising God is our priestly calling. And here is something even more profound: In the courts of the temple of Jerusalem there hung a four-inch-thick curtain that separated the people from the Most Holy Place where the presence of God lived. When Jesus died, the curtain was torn apart, top to bottom, by God Himself to show we now all have access to His presence.[10] (Remember our all-access pass?) That put an end to the bloody sacrifices God had required for two thousand years. Jesus changed everything! He gave us "confidence to enter the Most Holy Place . . . by a new and living way opened for us through the curtain, that is, his body" (Hebrews 10:19–20). So now as priests—and remember we all are priests—we have a new job! Here it is:

Through Jesus, therefore, let us continually
offer to God a sacrifice of praise—the fruit of lips
that openly profess his name.

HEBREWS 13:15

I love *The Message* translation: "Let's take our place outside with Jesus, no longer pouring out the sacrificial blood of animals but pouring out sacrificial praises from our lips to God in Jesus' name."

Now that we know we are "priests" and God has given us the job of praising Him, how exactly do we do that?

HOW TO PRACTICE PRAISE

When I was just beginning to read about and study the important and priestly work of worshiping God through praise, I met a wonderful man, Pastor Jack Taylor, who had a similar experience when the Lord directed him to preach about praise. He realized how little he knew, so he began to study and got excited about what he was learning. He then wrote a book called *The Hallelujah Factor*. I have been using his research for almost thirty years. I have also gleaned from the writings of Judson Cornwall, Ronald Allen, Gordon Borror, Mike Harland and Stan Moser, Travis Cottrell, Robin Mark, Warren and Ruth Myers, and others. I consulted Bible dictionaries and engaged in much personal practice. Praising and worshiping God is a lifelong exercise and should be a vital part of our journey toward heaven. And what a **joy** for us to learn more about this activity, then teach it to our children!

> Praising and worshiping God is a lifelong exercise and should be a vital part of our journey toward heaven. And what a **joy** for us to learn more about this activity, then teach it to our children!

Here are, in order, the seven most-used Hebrew words translated into English as "praise."[11] When there are small words in parenthesis like "both," "1st," and "all," it refers to the word "praise" being used more than once in the same verse. I realize this is a heavy list of verses, and reading so many at once may not be something you have done before. As you read them, ponder the actual meaning of God's specific direction from the original language. If you take some time to dig into God's Word, I think you will find, as I have, it deepens your understanding and causes you to know more of God revealed.

1. HALLAL (OR HALAL): "To be clear, shine, boast, rave, laud, celebrate, dance, leap, to be clamorously foolish, with reckless abandon!"

My favorite word, *hallelujah,* comes from *Hallal to Yahweh.* And everywhere you see "Hallelujah" written in the Bible, it is followed by an exclamation point! In English grammar, this is called an imperative—a command! I love to encourage people to change their thinking, to change their minds about praising God because it is something we **must do.** And when we hallelujah (*hallal*) to God, we put ourselves in position to receive from God.

Here is a more robust definition of *hallal*:

> To express great [in an extreme degree] or extravagant
> [spending much more than is necessary; excessive;
> exceeding the bounds of reason; going beyond
> what is justifiable; unrestrained] admiration
> [to regard with wonder, pleasure, approval].

In the following verses from the King James Version, *hallal* is translated into these English words:

A. **Praise:** 1 Chronicles 16:4, 23:5, 30, 25:3; 2 Chronicles 8:14, 20:21 (1st), 23:13, 29:30, 31:2; Psalm 22:22, 23, 26, 35:18, 56:4, 10 (both), 63:5, 69:30, 34, 74:21, 102:18, 104:35, 106:1, 48, 107:32, 111:1, 112:1, 113:1 (all), 9, 115:17, 18, 116:19, 117:1, 2, 119:164, 175, 135:1 (all), 3, 21, 145:2, 146:1 (both), 2 (1st), 10, 147:1 (1st), 12 (both), 20, 148 (all), 149:1, 3, 9; 150 (all); Jeremiah 20:13, 31:7; Joel 2:26.

B. **Praised:** 2 Samuel 22:4; 1 Chronicles 16:25, 36, 23:5; 2 Chronicles 5:13, 7:6, 20:19, 30:21; Psalm 18:3, 48:1, 96:4, 113:3, 145:3.

C. **Praises:** 2 Chronicles 29:30.

D. **Praising:** 2 Chronicles 5:13.

E. **Glory:** 1 Chronicles 16:10; Psalm 105:3, 106:5; Isaiah 41:16; Jeremiah 4:2, 9:24.

F. **Boast:** Psalm 34:2, 44:8.

2. YADAH: "To worship with extended hands, to throw out the hands giving thanks to God, lifting hands in surrender, commending a blessing with hands. This is the opposite of wringing the hands." It is used over ninety times in the Old Testament. The Hebrew word *yad* means "hand."

Jesus always used stories and examples so people would have mental pictures to better understand His teachings. This idea is not new, and *yadah* is one of those pictures. When we lift our hands we say, in essence, "I see You for who You are,

high and lifted up, and I place myself beneath You." Also we remind ourselves we are His children. A little child rarely comes
to us for love or for help without holding arms up to receive.
As a gesture of respect or commendation, we hold up our arms,
like a salute. Picture an army, a concert, or sports audience. That
is *yadah*.

In the King James Version *yadah* is translated as "give thanks"
thirty-two times, "thank" five times, and "confess" sixteen times.
In the following verses, *yadah* is translated into the English word:

Praise: 2 Chronicles 7:3, 6, 20:21 (both); Psalm 7:17
(both), 9:1, 28:7, 30:9, 33:2, 42:5, 11, 43:4, 5, 44:8,
45:17, 49:18, 52:9, 54:6, 67:3, 5, 71:22, 76:10, 86:12,
88:10, 89:5, 99:3, 107:8, 15, 21, 31, 108:3 (both), 109:30,
111:1 (both), 118:19, 21, 28, 119:7, 138:2, 145:10; Isaiah
12:1, Jeremiah 33:11 (both).

Genesis 29:35 records the occasion of the birth of Leah's
fourth son, whom she named "Judah," meaning "praise the Lord."
The word "praise" in that verse is *yadah*.

I first learned about this "hand raising" thing when I was in
college. While at home one weekend, I told my mother about all
I was learning, about how it is God's command and lifting hands
is a picture of surrender and childlikeness. She said, "Honey, that
is just so sweet and I'm glad you can do that. I am just not comfortable. That would feel so strange and awkward to me." So I
just stopped talking about it and waited on God. I figured if it
was important for her to raise her hands to God, then He would
show her.

Not long after our chat, she and my dad came down to Auburn University (where I attended, as had they) for a football game. The band played! The eagle flew! The crowd yelled! And the head cheerleader came out for the traditional chant and said into the microphone, "All right, everybody! Get your hands up for a big WAR EAGLE!" (It's an Auburn thing.) So eighty thousand people raised their hands. So did my mom. She later told me she sensed the Lord asking, *What are you doing?* And she thought, *Well, I'm doin' a War Eagle!* And the Lord said, *So it's okay for you to raise your hands to a football team, but not to Me?* You should see my mama today. Every Sunday she sits in her pew at her Presbyterian church and raises her hands in front of God and everybody!

3. **BARAUCH (BARAK):** "To kneel, bless, salute, bow as an act of adoration, or humble submission."

The following English words are translated from the Hebrew word *barauch* in the King James Version:

- **A. Bless:** Psalm 16:7, 66:8, 96:2, 100:4, 103:1, 2, 20–22, 104:1, 35, 135:19, 20.
- **B. Blessed:** Exodus 18:10; Ruth 4:14; 1 Samuel 25:32, 39; 2 Samuel 18:28; 1 Kings 1:48, 5:7, 8:15, 56, 10:9; 1 Chronicles 16:36; 2 Chronicles 2:12, 6:4, 9:8, 20:26; Ezra 7:27; Nehemiah 8:6; Job 1:21; Psalm 18:46, 31:21, 41:13, 66:20, 68:19, 35, 72:18, 19 (both), 89:52, 106:48, 119:12, 124:6, 135:21, 144:1; Ezekiel 3:12; Daniel 2:20, 3:28, 4:34.
- **C. Kneel:** Psalm 95:6.

In Scripture, we are instructed to "bless" (*barauch*) the Father:

- at all times (Psalm 34:1).
- as long as we live (Psalm 63:4).
- from day to day (Psalm 96:2).
- forever and ever, every day (Psalm 115:18).
- at night in the house of the Lord (Psalm 134:1).
- from this time forth and forever (Psalm 145:1–2).

I had the privilege of visiting Jerusalem a few years ago. At the Western Wall I watched the many men who prayed there and noticed their posture. Most held their Bibles or prayer books, faced the wall, and bowed as they prayed. This is the idea of *barauch*.

4. TEHILLAH: "To sing with, by, or in the Spirit, the singing of *hallals*."

Tehillah is translated in English in the King James Version only as:

Praise: Exodus 15:11; Deuteronomy 10:21; 1 Chronicles 16:35; 2 Chronicles 20:22; Nehemiah 9:5, 12:46; Psalm 9:14, 22:3, 25, 33:1, 34:1, 35:28, 40:3, 48:10, 51:15, 65:1, 66:2, 8, 71:6, 8, 14, 79:13, 100:4, 102:21, 106:2, 12, 47, 111:10, 119:171, 145:21, 147:1 (2nd), 148:14 (1st), 149:1 (2nd); Isaiah 61:3.

If you know me or have ever seen Miss PattyCake, you can see how committed I am to *tehillah*. Remember my encouragement to sing your way through your day? That's because *tehillah* puts us in the presence of God. Psalm 22:3 (KJV) says, "But thou art holy, O thou that inhabitest the [*tehillah*] of Israel." When we are where God lives, we are in His presence. I don't know about you, but I want to live like that. HALLELUJAH!

5. ZAMAR: "To touch the strings, playing instruments, to make music accompanied by the voice. To celebrate. To sing songs of praise with instruments."

Zamar is translated in the King James Version as:

> **A. Praise:** Psalm 57:7, 9, 108:1, 138:1 (both).
> **B. Sing Praise(s):** Psalm 7:17, 9:2, 11, 18:49, 27:6, 47:6 (all), 61:8, 92:1, 108:3, 135:3, 144:9, 146:2, 147:1, 149:3.
> **C. Sing:** Psalm 30:4, 12, 33:2, 57:9, 59:17, 61:8, 66:2, 4 (both), 71:22, 23, 75:9, 98:4, 5; Isaiah 12:5.
> **D. Sing Psalms:** 1 Chronicles 16:9; Psalm 105:2.

Here are some great examples of the attitude of *zamar*. It is very interesting to me that the Lord is so specific to tell us that he likes hearing stringed instruments. I know a man who plays the harp beautifully. At his concerts he stands and says, "Praise the Lord with the harp!" (see Psalm 98:5), then sits and plays. I like picturing God and Jesus smiling and clapping along.

> *Sing to the L*ORD *with grateful praise;*
> *make music* [zamar] *to our God on the harp.*
> PSALM 147:7

It is good to praise [yadah] *the LORD,*
and make music [zamar] *to your name, O Most High,*
proclaiming your love in the morning
and your faithfulness at night,
to the music of the ten-stringed lyre
and the melody of the harp.

PSALM 92:1–3

Make music [zamar] *to the LORD with the harp,*
with the harp and the sound of singing,
with trumpets and the blast of the ram's horn—
shout for joy before the LORD, the King.

PSALM 98:5–6

Praise [barauch] *be to the LORD my Rock,*
who trains my hands for war, my fingers for battle. . . .
I will sing a new song to you, my God;
on the ten-stringed lyre I will
make music [zamar] *to you.*

PSALM 144:1, 9

6. SHABACH: "To proclaim in a loud voice, shout, commend, bless, declare. A loud adoration, the testimony of what God has done, a joyful to overflowing attitude."

Shabach is translated in the King James Version as:

A. Praise: Psalm 63:3, 106:47, 117:1 (both), 145:4, 147:12 (both).
B. Shout: Psalm 32:11, 47:1, 100:1.

Over and over again we are told to shout, to be loud, and most theologians agree it is a powerful weapon in spiritual warfare. While there are only a few places where *shabach* is translated as "praise," there are many places God commands a "shout." Below are two powerful verses associated with *shabach*.

> *But let all who take refuge in You be glad,*
> *let them ever sing for joy;*
> *and may You shelter them,*
> *that those who love Your name may exult in You.*
>
> PSALM 5:11 [NASB]

. . . .

> *When the builders laid the foundation of the temple*
> *of the LORD, the priests in their vestments and with trumpets,*
> *and the Levites (the sons of Asaph) with cymbals,*
> *took their places to praise the LORD, as prescribed*
> *by David king of Israel. With praise and thanksgiving*
> *they sang to the LORD: "He is good, his love toward*
> *Israel endures forever." And all the people gave*
> *a great shout of praise to the LORD, because*
> *the foundation of the house of the LORD was laid.*
>
> EZRA 3:10-11

YAHOO! I love *shabach*! So do children. When I do live events, I always give them permission to use their "outside voices." There is power in shouting. When someone shouts you know he means business. Jesus shouted in righteous anger at the merchants in the temple. The word *shabach* is like the word *hallal* and is often written with an exclamation point. That makes it a command. So DO IT!

7. TODAH (TOWDAH): "To extend the hands in a sacrifice of praise, thanksgiving, or thank-offering. Also, to thank in advance for things not yet visible: a faith praise."

Todah is translated in the King James Version as:

A. **Praise:** Psalm 42:4, 50:23; Jeremiah 17:26, 33:11 (both).
B. **Praises:** Psalm 56:12, 68:4, 32, 75:9.
C. **Thanks:** Nehemiah 12:31, 38, 40.
D. **Thanksgiving:** Leviticus 22:29; Psalm 26:7, 50:14, 69:30, 95:2, 107:22, 116:17, 147:7; Isaiah 51:3; Jeremiah 30:19; Amos 4:5.

This faith praise moves God:

> *He who offers a sacrifice of praise*
> *and thanksgiving honors Me;*
> *And to him who orders his way rightly*
> *[who follows the way that I show him],*
> *I shall show the salvation of God.*
> PSALM 50:23 (AMP)

Sing to God, sing in praise of his name,
extol him who rides on the clouds;
rejoice before him—his name is the LORD.

PSALM 68:4

Let us come before him with thanksgiving [todah]
and extol him with music and song.

PSALM 95:2

Praise *(todah)* honors God, and this specific praise, which is a sacrificial offering, is important because it contains *faith.* Sometimes we have to put our understanding of things aside and give thanks and praise regardless of our situation. That is a *sacrifice of praise,* trusting God in the circumstance. Giving thanks to God is the natural response to knowing Him and appreciating all He has given.

The book of Jonah tells the story of one such sacrifice. Jonah disobeyed God, then tried to run away from God. Big mistake! He got in a boat, provoked a storm, was thrown overboard and swallowed by a big fish. Inside the fish, he had time to consider his actions and decided to offer a **sacrifice of praise**: "'But I, with shouts of grateful praise [*todah*], will sacrifice to you. What I have vowed I will make good. I will say, "Salvation comes from the LORD." And the LORD commanded the fish, and it vomited Jonah onto dry land'" (Jonah 2:9–10).

Leviticus 22:29 (NKJV) uses *todah* this way: "And when you offer a sacrifice of thanksgiving [*todah*] to the Lord, offer it of your own free will." Jesus offered a sacrifice of thanksgiving of his own free will just before He was crucified. He "took bread, gave *thanks* and broke it, and gave it to them" (Luke 22:19, emphasis mine). This word is translated "thanks" from the Greek word *eucharisteo* and is actually three words in one: *charis* meaning "grace," *chara* meaning "joy," and *eucharisteo* meaning "thanksgiving."[12] Certainly Jesus's thanksgiving on this occasion was a **sacrifice** to God since He knew He was about to die on the cross. Jesus gave **thanks** by **grace** with **joy**. I love the way Ann Voskamp voices her understanding of this idea: "*Eucharisteo*—thanksgiving—always precedes the miracle."[13] The giving of thanks and praise by **faith** comes before salvation. Like Jonah and Jesus, you and I can offer *todah* praise in the face of difficulties and watch for God's salvation!

> There are many ways to give God praise and He is pleased with all of them.

MIX IT UP

One of the first verses I remember learning, probably in Vacation Bible School (thank you, Dawson Memorial Baptist in Birmingham, Alabama) was Psalm 100. It is considered a psalm for giving thanks and uses an interesting combination of Hebrew words for "praise" in verse 4: "Enter his gates with thanksgiving [*todah*] and his courts with praise [*tehillah*]: give thanks [*yadah*] to him and praise [*barauch*] his name."

You may be thinking, *That kind of outward expression of thanks works for you. You're comfortable wearing that costume, you are naturally uninhibited, and you probably didn't grow up in a quiet, conservative church the way I did.*

Be encouraged by these words from the great conservative reformer, John Calvin:

> The stability of the world depends on this rejoicing of God in His works. If on earth, such praise of God does not come to pass . . . then the whole order of nature will be thrown into confusion. We are cold when it comes to rejoicing in God! Hence, we need to exercise ourselves in it and employ all our senses in it—our feet, our hands, our arms and all the rest—that they all might serve in the worship of God and so magnify Him.[14]

Exercise yourself and your children/grandchildren in the **praise of God**! There are many ways to give God praise, and He is pleased with all of them. Now that you know more about praise, you may find yourself enjoying new expressions of praise to God in your own life.

CHILDLIKE PRAISE

Have you noticed how easy it is for children to sing, shout, dance, clap, jump? Are you jealous? I am! Children are generally uninhibited. They do not overthink. As Miss PattyCake I see this all the time. I have observed that children require no great logic or apologetics when you talk about God; you just have to tell them His name. Simply say, "Jesus. The One you can't see. The One who made you and loves you." Often they say, "Oh, Him!"

How can they know this so early?

Ecclesiastes 3:11 says God "set eternity in the human heart." The Amplified Bible translation further explains that God "planted eternity [a sense of divine purpose] in the human heart [a mysterious longing which nothing under the sun can satisfy, except God]."

Note also the great Blaise Pascal wrote much about theology and philosophy, and *Pensées* was published posthumously in 1670 as a collection of assembled notes, fragments, and short essays-in-progress Pascal directed to his skeptical and restless friends. Hoping to move them to seek God, he wrote,

> There is a God shaped vacuum
> in the heart of every man
> which cannot be filled by any created thing,
> but only by God, the Creator,
> made known through Jesus.[15]

We can begin early to fill that "vacuum" with the Word of God and with His **praises!**

• •

> *From the lips of children and infants you,*
> *Lord, have called forth your praise.*

MATTHEW 21:16

• •

HOW TO *PULL* PRESCHOOLERS INTO PRAISE

P = PRAY Ask God for help.

U = UNDERSTANDING You now know seven different types of praise and how to practice praise with your children, grandchildren, class, or little friends.

L = LEVEL Try to think on their level. Remember they have to crawl before walking and walk before running. They need milk before meat. Find simple, age-appropriate songs, stories, and activities that teach and practice praise. By the way, Miss PattyCake can help with that!

L = LOVE We already feel love for the children in our care, but love is also a verb . . . something we choose to **do**. We love God by praising, thanking, obeying, and serving Him. Jesus asked Peter, "Do you love me? Feed my lambs" (see John 21:15–17). You are loving God and loving your children/grandchildren when you practice praise with them!

Are you ready to "get some praise on," to trade your burdens, your frustrations, and your fears for some **joy**? Praise! Does that seem too simple? Can the feeling of joy really come easily when we practice praise and give thanks? Ann Voskamp, mother of seven, gives this thought:

> I hold my head in my hands and ask it honestly before God and children and my daily mess: *Can we really expect joy all the time*? . . . I may feel disappointment and the despair may flood high, but to *give thanks* is an

action and *rejoice* is a verb and these are not mere pulsing emotions. While I may not always feel joy, God asks me to give thanks in all things because He knows that the feeling of joy begins in the action of thanksgiving. JOY—it's always obedience.[16]

· ·

Rejoice in the Lord always.
I will say it again: Rejoice!
PHILIPPIANS 4:4

· ·

After reading this chapter, I hope you have learned something new. My experience of teaching these biblical truths about praise for more than thirty years has proven that this knowledge is **powerful**. Hosea 4:6 says, "My people are destroyed from lack of knowledge." Today you have armed yourself with life-giving knowledge from the Word of God, which can empower you to better understand and practice a life of praise. Psalm 90:14 (NLT) says, "Satisfy us each morning with your unfailing love, so we may sing for joy to the end of our lives."

Now take a deep breath, raise your hands, and shout . . .

HALLELUJAH!

GIGGLE BREAK

My sister took my young nephew to church for children's choir. She was excited for him and hoped he would, like most of our musical family, love it! She waited by the room for dismissal, then asked him, "So was it fun? Did you like it? Did you like the teacher?" He was nonchalant. "It was okay. We played games and had a snack. My teacher is nice and there was music. The only thing I didn't like was the singing."

E

Chapter 6

ENTHUSIASTIC ENJOYMENT

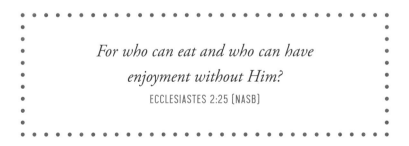

*For who can eat and who can have
enjoyment without Him?*
ECCLESIASTES 2:25 [NASB]

Did you know the very word *enthusiasm* is rooted in God? It comes directly from the Latin word *enthūsiasmus* and the Greek term *enthousiasmós,* which means "divine inspiration, enthusiasm, inspired or, be rapt, be in ecstasy, fever or zeal (produced by certain kinds of music, etc.)." It also comes from *entheos: en* meaning "in" + *theos* meaning "god." So being enthusiastic literally means being "in god."[1] Ecclesiastes 2:25 speaks of finding enjoyment *in God!* We see this also in 1 Timothy 6:17 (NLT), "Teach those who are rich in this world not to be proud and not to trust in their money, which is so unreliable. Their trust should be in God, who richly gives us all we need for our *enjoyment"* (emphasis mine). The Bible is full of these refreshing words: joy, gladness, rejoicing, and celebration. In God we can have *enthusiastic enjoyment!*

• • • • • • • • • • • • •

The Bible is full of these refreshing words: joy, gladness, rejoicing, and celebration.
In God we can have *enthusiastic enjoyment!*

• • • • • • • • • • • • •

Miss PattyCake rounded a corner and almost bumped into a three-year-old boy. He looked up at me and screamed! (I'm used to this.) Assuming he was afraid of me in a costume, I dropped to one knee and said, "Hi there!" with a big smile. He backed up a little, never taking his eyes off me, and said loudly,

"HOW DID YOU GET OUT OF MY TV?" I fell over laughing. I love my job!

I love to laugh . . . especially when something surprises me. You probably know that when we laugh our brains release those feel-good endorphins, which can remind us to thank the Lord for His gift of *funny* in this world. "A cheerful heart is good medicine," says Proverbs 17:22. God knew we would need laughter in our lives to keep us healthy and mentally strong. The Mayo Clinic lists these benefits to laughing as often as possible:

SHORT-TERM BENEFITS: LAUGHTER

- **Stimulates many organs.** Laughter stimulates your heart, lungs, and muscles.
- **Activates and relieves your stress response.** A boisterous laugh fires up, then cools down your stress response, increasing your heart rate and blood pressure, which gives you a relaxed feeling.
- **Soothes tension.** Laughter can also stimulate circulation and aid muscle relaxation.

LONG-TERM BENEFITS: LAUGHTER

- **Improves your immune system.** Positive thoughts and laughter actually release neuropeptides that help fight stress and potentially more serious illnesses.
- **Relieves pain.** Laughter may ease pain by causing the body to produce its own natural painkillers.
- **Increases personal satisfaction.** Laughter can make it easier to cope with difficult situations. It also helps you connect with other people.

- **Improves your mood.** Laughter can help lessen your depression and anxiety and may make you feel happier.[2]

I have a crazy, adorable friend named Marilyn Meberg. She's a giggler, and one of the best storytellers you will ever meet. She wrote a fabulous book called *I'd Rather Be Laughing*,[3] which is full of hilarious stories and research on the positive, healthy effects of laughter. I recommend you find it and read it with a box of tissues nearby—you'll need them to wipe your eyes. For a whole year she did a "laugh test" at the Women of Faith conferences. She stood in the arena and started laughing—at nothing. She just began with a giggle, then it grew into a guffaw, became a loud "HA HA HA," then she started slapping her knee and bent double just howling . . . at herself! Most every woman in the arena was laughing at her, at each other, and at the laughter! It felt fabulous and ridiculous at the same time.

Laughter is contagious! And what a fun exercise to do with children—get them laughing. They don't need much coaxing, as you already know. They naturally laugh at most anything. I sing a cute song at all my concerts called, "Wiggly, Giggly" and it is a blast watching children sing it. Before we start to sing I say, "Can you follow my directions? Wiggle your fingers, now wiggle your toes, wiggle your shoulders, and wiggle your nose. Now giggle and wiggle and giggle some more!" And they are laughing and wiggling and parents are laughing with them and at them and then we finish and everyone is smiling and feeling happy and it's great fun!

Don't you love finding fun in your life? I hope you do. I look for it regularly because I believe we are supposed to glorify God and enjoy Him forever! It could be I am brainwashed . . .

In every job that must be done
There is an element of fun
You find the fun and snap!
The job's a game.[4]

Did you picture Mary Poppins? Did you hear Julie Andrews's voice in your head? She was my childhood hero. I wanted to *be* her—mostly just to sing all those songs in the film and jump inside the sidewalk picture. Oh, and ride those carousel horses, dance with Bert, and sit upside down on the ceiling singing, "I Love to Laugh"! Then I wanted to "Feed the Birds" and fall asleep to the song "Stay Awake." Then I'd sing "Supercalifragilisticexpialidocious" and "Let's Go Fly a Kite"!

You know what I love about that movie? There is variety in the music and the story—fast, slow, sweet, silly, a little scary, working songs, love songs. We are multifacted, emotional creatures and we can be touched by and learn from all sorts of experiences. God our Creator, in whose image we are made, is also multifaceted. I love what Romans 1:20 says about Him:

For since the creation of the world
God's invisible qualities—his eternal power
and divine nature—have been clearly seen,
being understood from what has been made,
so that people are without excuse.

Miss PattyCake sings this song called "Colors, Numbers, ABCs":

Everywhere we look we see
In colors, numbers, ABCs
Everywhere we look we see
God loves you and God loves me.[5]

We look, we smell, we taste, we touch, we hear, and we experience the varied experience of God's creativity! And there are so many ways to point these out to our little ones. I've mentioned a book about creativity I like called *The Artist's Way for Parents*. Here is a great suggestion from it: "Many mothers and fathers reach day's end tired— and even crabby. Tucking their child into bed, they are ready for the day to be over. But bedtime can be a time of restorative ritual. Highlight your day to end it on a positive note. Ask, 'What was your favorite part of our day?' A child loves to chat about these things. Your child may reply, 'I liked swinging.' The habit of looking for the positive is something that makes each day's march into a game. Use bedtime conversation to review the day's happy highlights and it will forge joyful memories for your child."[6]

> The habit of looking for the positive is something that makes each day's march into a game.

GOD AND GROCERIES

I like to eat, which means I cook, and therefore I must grocery shop. I don't hate the grocery store (especially when they give samples). The relaxing music at my favorite store always slows me down, so I look at people around me. Lately I have seen more and more parents who do this: *Walk in . . . child on hip or by the hand . . . pull out cart . . . plunk child in cart . . . reach for phone or iPad or any device with a screen . . . touch On . . . give device to child . . . shop . . . no talking.*

Have you seen this? Have you done this? Believe me, I get it! We are busy! We have stuff to do, meals to cook, clothes to wash, meetings to attend, calls to make, groceries to buy, coupons to use, money to save, homes to return to, groceries to put away, food to cook, dishes to do, bedtime routines—it's all go, go, go.

• • • • • • • • • •

A great adventure
in parenting is
looking for
and finding
God *everywhere*.

• • • • • • • • • •

But if we pause and take a minute to breathe, we might see our grocery trip as an opportunity, a creative time to talk to our children about the Lord. Deuteronomy 6:7 instructs us to talk about Him when we sit at home, when we walk along the road, when we get up in the morning, when we lie down at night. And that means even when we are at the grocery store! Remember Romans 1:20, "God's invisible qualities . . . have been clearly seen, being understood from what has been made. "

So what does this have to do with grocery shopping? It's a good time to pay attention to what has been made! As you walk through the produce, notice shapes and colors.

Tell your children/grandchildren, "God made this."

Have them touch, smell, and see. Thank God for eyes, fingers, and a nose.

Feel a potato, touch an onion, smell some fennel.

"What do you see that is orange? Can you find something yellow?"

Play "I spy."

Have them close their eyes and smell mint, rosemary, basil, or cilantro.

Tell them, "Thank God for your tongue. We can taste all the good food He has made!"

Go to the dairy case. Ask, "Where do we get milk and eggs?" Thank God for cows and hens, and farmers.

Make animal noises. Go ahead . . . embarrass yourself! Your kids will **love it**! (I should know. I dress in a costume and embarrass my kids all the time!)

A great adventure in parenting is looking for and finding God *everywhere*. So, were all my trips to the grocery a glorious parenting experience? HA! No. I always hope for successful teaching moments, even the time my  son knocked over a display and sent jars of spaghetti sauce crashing. What a mess. But I put on a brave face and said, "Wow! Red is EVERYWHERE!" *Cleanup on aisle three. . . .*

REMEMBER TO HAVE FUN

Sometime in my early thirties BC (Before Children), I attended a beach retreat and happened to be hanging out with the speaker, who was a pastor. We were having a nice conversation when he spotted his kids and sternly yelled, "Hey, come here!" I was shocked this man would speak to his children that way, and right in front of me and others. They ran over and he grabbed each by one arm and angrily said, "Now you two listen to me! You are going to be in big trouble, BIG TROUBLE. Do you hear me?"

The two children nodded and were smiling. I was confused.

"We are leaving right now and going home IF you do not have the BEST TIME OF YOUR LIFE! Now go out there and have FUN OR ELSE!" They laughed and ran off to play.

Whew! I was relieved, and we all laughed. What a performance! We all thought he was angry, but I realized his kids had seen it all before. I have never forgotten that moment. That guy was just plain silly. He knew how to make things fun. He practiced **enthusiastic enjoyment**!

I heard about this one: It was a hot day and a family went to get ice cream. They walked out with those yummy, sticky ice-cream cones, and the three-year-old promptly dropped his on the sidewalk. He let out a wail. Daddy to the rescue! "Quick! Take off your shoes!" The crying little boy looked up, confused. "Take off your shoes and step in it!" Those tears dried up! The little guy put his bare toes in that cold stuff and began to giggle. He squished it around, howled with laughter, and made a huge mess. I'm sure the mommy was digging in her bag for some wipes, but the dad's creativity saved the day. Everyone had a great time watching, and it made a memory of laughter. That is joy in the journey.

One day in my kitchen in Mobile, Alabama, I had a girl-friend over and we were chatting while I cleaned. Four-year-old Marilyn was playing in her room and two-year old Christopher was in the backyard swinging a stick. Marilyn proudly came into the kitchen showing us her new crown, dress, and little high-heeled plastic shoes. I should have taken a picture. Her brother walked in just at that moment. She looked at him, twirled, and said, "Look at me! I'm a princess!"

That little two-year-old boy looked at her, raised his stick, and yelled, "KILL THE PRINCESS!"

She screamed, he yelled, and a chase ensued. I thought I would die laughing. I mean, really? Who taught him to say that? That was unexpected hilarity, and I still smile when I remember it.

One of my favorite laugh-worthy moments: A mother invited some people to dinner. At the table, she turned to her five-year-old daughter and asked, "Would you like to say the blessing?"

"I don't know what to say," the girl replied.

"Just say what you hear Mommy say."

The daughter bowed her head and said, "Lord, why on earth did I invite all these people to dinner?"

COPYCAT

Little children are imitators. They watch every move and copy our attitude and actions. Children are mirrors of our lives. That should terrify us! You know, in a good way it should make us more aware of consequences from our words and actions.

Did you ever play copycat? I did—a lot! I am the oldest of four children and my father was a traveling salesman. We went on road trips often and there was no TV, no DVD player, no cell phone, no hand-held electronic *anything* in the car. We played games. "I spy " for miles, "copycat" until our mama begged us for the "quiet game."

When I perform the "Copycat" song at a Miss PattyCake

concert, I always like to refer to the verse Ephesians 5:1 (ESV): "Therefore be imitators of God, as beloved children." "Imitator" is a big word for a little person, and often the best way to explain a word is to show them. "Here—imitate this, do what I do . . . be a copycat." Jesus did this all the time. He told stories, He used illustrations, and probably He played games with the children. (I like to think He did.)

The next time you are trying to teach your children something new, start with Miss PattyCake's "Copycat" song to get their attention:

> *This and that, copy cat,*
> *Whatever I do you do it, too.*
> *It's a little game where we do the same . . .*
> *Okay—here we go!*
> *Pat your head, swing your arms around,*
> *Shake your shoulders, up and down.*
> *Pat your tummy, count to three*
> *Clap together and sing with me![7]*

Little children love to play games, especially if music is involved. So sing this little song, play the game, and ask your children to copy you as *you* copy Jesus. Jesus went about doing good. He walked in love. So now you and your children are living the very next verse!

> *Walk in the way of love, just as Christ loved us and gave himself up for us as a fragrant offering and sacrifice to God.*
> EPHESIANS 5:2

The Message translation puts it this way:

> *Watch what God does, and then you do it, like children*
> *who learn proper behavior from their parents. Mostly what*
> *God does is love you. Keep company with him and learn*
> *a life of love. Observe how Christ loved us.*
> *His love was not cautious but extravagant. He didn't love*
> *in order to get something from us but to give everything*
> *of himself to us. Love like that.*
> EPHESIANS 5:1–2

See? It's all about being a copycat. How do we copy God? We look at the life of Jesus. He said, "If you really know me, you will know my Father as well" (John 14:7). Read what Jesus did, and you'll learn that He mostly just loved people. He went about doing good and, helping others. I like to look at the word "therefore" to find what it is *there for*. It usually refers to whatever came right before it. Ephesians 4:32 comes before the "Therefore be imitators" of 5:1 and says,

> *Be kind and compassionate to one another,*
> *forgiving each other, just as in Christ God forgave you.*

Let's copy **that**! If we as parents will ask the Father to create this lifestyle of love, kindness, and forgiveness in us, our children will see it and naturally copy us as we instruct them. Together we will copy Jesus!

I realize, in the hullabaloo[8] of life with babies, toddlers, and/or preschoolers, this is easier said than done. In the seemingly

> If we as parents will ask the Father to create this lifestyle of love, kindness, and forgiveness in us, our children will see it and naturally copy us as we instruct them. Together we will copy Jesus!

endless diapers, bottles, sippy cups and spills, messy play areas, crayons, snacks, mountains of laundry, dishes, and going, going, going, take a moment—breathe—look up—**thank God** in all of it and remember this: "For it is God who works in you both to *will* and to *do* for His good pleasure" (Philippians 2:13 NKJV, emphasis mine).

That, my friend, is the **key**. It takes the pressure off us to do it all ourselves . . . to always get it all right. Parenting and caring are God's work *in* us and *through* us. Can we love our children well? He can love them well *through us.* Can we always be kind? Can we always forgive? God the Holy Spirit is alive in us and, as we give Him permission, He lives that beautiful love life *through us* and it spills onto our little ones. **Copy that!**

IDEAS WORTH IMITATING

- **Practice Gratitude.** Give thanks in *all* things (see Colossians 3:16–17).
- **Practice Prayer.** Call on Jesus *out loud***. . . .** Ask, seek, knock (see Matthew 7:7).
- **Practice Serving.** Do service projects *with* your kids because "faith without deeds is dead," (James 2:26).
- **Practice Bible Memory.** Learn scripture *together*, sing the Word, pray scriptures back to God. "I have hidden your word in my heart" (Psalm 119:11).

- **Practice Family Worship.** *Make time* to thank, praise, teach, and worship the Lord as a family (see Deuteronomy 6:6–7).

NOTHING IS TOO SMALL

It was a normal busy day. My kids were little and we were going . . . somewhere. I buckled Christopher into the car seat, ran back in the house to grab my purse, gather stuff, and hurry Marilyn along. I opened my purse to get the car keys. Not there. I rushed into the kitchen to look on the counter. Not there. Were they on the dresser in the bedroom? Not there. I looked in the bathroom, the closet, and again in the living room. Now I was really frustrated! Before I became frantic I yelled, "LORD JESUS! WHERE ARE MY KEYS?" Then I stopped, closed my eyes, and waited. It took a few seconds, but into my mind came the picture of my jacket lying over a chair in my daughter's room—right where I'd left it yesterday—with my keys in the pocket. "Thank You!" I grabbed those keys and we were on our way. (The Holy Spirit is brilliant!)

A few days later we were headed out again and I instructed Marilyn to find her shoes. Soon I heard her three-year old voice loudly say, "LORD JESUS! WHERE ARE MY SHOES?"

Are you convinced God cares about your life? Your answer is likely yes. But I actually mean your *whole* life—the daily stuff, the everyday cleaning, shopping, cooking, working, eating, drinking, dressing, playing, walking around, have-to-get-it-done life. Have you embraced the idea that God wants to live all of that life **with** you and give you joy in this journey? Just in case you have listened to the lie that God is somehow too busy to be bothered with the little things, let me remind you how much He cares. He knows exactly how many hairs are on our heads (see Luke 12:7; Matthew 10:30). He even knows a word before we speak it (Psalm 139:4). Those things may seem little to us, and we know with babies, toddlers, and preschoolers, life is full of little stuff. It all matters to our children, and it all matters to God.

. . . .

So here's what I want you to do, God helping you:
Take your everyday, ordinary life—your sleeping, eating,
going-to-work, and walking-around life—and place it
before God as an offering. Embracing what God does for
you is the best thing you can do for him. Don't become
so well-adjusted to your culture that you fit into it without
even thinking. Instead, fix your attention on God.
You'll be changed from the inside out. Readily recognize
what he wants from you, and quickly respond to it.
Unlike the culture around you, always dragging you down
to its level of immaturity, God brings the best out of you,
develops well-formed maturity in you.

ROMANS 12:1–2 (MSG)

. . . .

PATTYCAKE DAILY IDEAS
PUT ON A PRESCHOOL FACE

Your face—eyes open, inviting smile—can communicate God's love. Make a point to be happy to see them. Try this: "I'm so glad to see your face this morning," or "YAY—you are here!" Let your love and attention show on your face.

My children attended a mother's-day-out program once a week when they were about two and three. I can't remember the name of the woman who greeted us, but I can still see her smiling face and hear her voice because she always said the same thing to my children: "Hey, my loves." On paper this doesn't look the way it sounded to my ears, but my children always wanted to go. They felt loved. Thank you, precious grandmother at Cottage Hill Baptist in Mobile, Alabama, for loving my children!

GET ON THEIR LEVEL

Okay . . . you might have to get on your knees for this. Can you get your face close to theirs? Take time to make eye contact. Go on, sit in that little chair, get down on your knees, grab a pillow if you must, pull them into your lap. The floor really is your friend.

I love when I get hand-drawn, usually crayon pictures from my little friends. Almost without fail they picture Miss PattyCake with big feet, looonnnggg legs, and a little triangle for a dress. They try to draw the red heart, but it is usually a lump. Loonngg arms with sticky-outy fingers, a small round head, a hat, and a huge red mouth (it's the lipstick). I have a collection of these fabulous pictures. This is the way they see me . . . I'm tall, and onstage I seem even taller. They are far from my face. But *you* can get on their level.

> Have you embraced the idea that God wants to live all of life **with** you and give you joy in this journey?

HAVE RITUALS

Repetition and structure help communicate a sense of security. I grew up with Mr. Rogers. I loved that he always, **always** sang the same greeting song as he changed from a coat to a sweater, switched his shoes, and said, "Hi, neighbor." His structure was comforting to me and I anticipated what came next. Start with the children in *your* care. You can say every day, "This is the day God has made!" Choose a theme song. By the way, they don't care whether you sing well, and neither does God. Here are ideas for daily structure:

- Story time
- Prayer time
- Check the weather
- Play time
- Nap time
- Snack time
- Exploring (nature walk, read an I Spy book)
- Game time.

Little children thrive on repetition. Anticipate being reminded about leaving anything out!

LET THEM EXPLORE

Ask them questions. Don't tell them everything . . . let them tell you. Act surprised when you hear a common sound (doorbell, telephone, thunder, baby crying, dog barking, car horn). Then ask, "What was that?" Ask your children, "What is God like?" and "What does God say?" You may be surprised and touched by their answers. They often give us insight we are too big to see.

Use the phrase, "I wonder . . ." to help children think, respond, and problem-solve. For example, "I wonder what we should do about all these dirty dishes?" Children are born with an abundance of curiosity—but I'm not telling you anything new. You know they seem to constantly ask, "When, where, why, how, what?" They believe everything is possible—they don't make assumptions. They swim in the sea of possibilities. Shouldn't we all be like that? Jesus said,

> *"Truly I tell you, unless you change*
> *and become like little children,*
> *you will never enter the kingdom of heaven."*
> MATTHEW 18:3

SILENCE IS GOOD

Whisper to get their attention. Encourage them to learn how to listen for God. Have a designated quiet time and practice being still. That's not easy for most children, but you can make a game of it. Begin with little bits of time . . . thirty seconds can seem long to them. Ask your child to make their toes be quiet, then legs, then arms, then head, then mouth. You may find it helps both of you.

LISTEN

Pay attention to the details of their lives. Most children want to talk. They want to talk about *everything*. They are figuring stuff out as they talk: "I fell down yesterday, see my Band-Aid?" "We went to the store." "Mommy got mad." "Logan hit me." "I don't like carrots." When we listen, we become a friend. And oh my, the things you may hear. Our attention communicates love.

MUSIC IS MAGICAL

Sing songs about everything. I probably say too much about this . . . but it is true and it works. Music is like glue; it makes words stick to our brains. What happens in your mind when you hear these words: "I am stuck on Band-Aids, 'cause a Band-Aid's stuck on me!" How about "My bologna has a first name" or "Like a good neighbor . . . "? Did you finish that line? Could you hear the music in your head? Why? Because it is music—and music lives in our brains in an indelible way.

Many of my earliest memories are musical. My mother tells stories of me at age three singing "Jesus Loves Me" at the top of my lungs to anyone who would listen—at the grocery store, at the gas station, out the window to passersby. I would lie in bed at night and recount the events of the day in a spontaneous, made-up song.

Later, as a mother of preschoolers, I always looked for a way to make "the job a game." And my method was always **music!** (Mary Poppins helped.) Have you seen all the music products available for our babies? They guarantee mathematical and scientific aptitude. They tell us to play music and see a child's vocabulary increase, prepare them for school, even teach them to read. Companies promote all kinds of music for little ones— even music for babies in utero. As I mentioned earlier, scientific research tells us there is something "magical" about music.[9]

> Music is like glue;
> it makes words
> stick to our brains.

Look at this research:

Music speaks in a language that children instinctively understand. It draws children (as well as adults) into its orbit, inviting them to match its pitches, incorporate its lyrics, move to its beat, and explore its emotional and harmonic dimensions in all their beauty and depth. Meanwhile, its physical vibrations, organized patterns, engaging rhythms, and subtle variations interact with the mind and body in manifold ways, naturally altering the brain in a manner that one-dimensioned rote learning cannot. Children are happy when they are bouncing, dancing, clapping, and singing with someone they trust and love. Even as music delights and entertains them, it helps mold their mental, emotional, social, and physical development—and gives them the enthusiasm and the skills they need to begin to teach themselves.[10]

Another word from the ancient teacher/philosopher, Plato: "I would teach children music, physics, and philosophy; but most importantly music, for the patterns in music and all the arts are the keys to learning."[11]

BENEFITS OF USING MUSIC WITH CHILDREN

- It can connect with them even before birth.
- It stimulates brain growth in the womb and throughout early childhood.

- It positively affects emotional perceptions and attitudes from prebirth onward.

- It provides patterns of sound on which they can build an understanding of the physical world.

- It reduces the level of emotional stress or physical pain, even in infancy.

- It enhances motor development, including the grace and ease with which they learn to crawl, walk, skip, and run.

- It improves language ability, including vocabulary, expressiveness, and ease of communication.

- It introduces them to a wider world of emotional expression, creativity, and aesthetic beauty.

- It enhances social abilities.

- It improves reading, writing, mathematical, and other academic skills, as well as the ability to remember and to memorize.

- It introduces them to the joys of community.

- It helps create a strong sense of personal identity.[12]

Author Don Campbell writes:

It is amazing to think that music and rhythmic verbal sounds, which have been available to us throughout our lives, can have such a powerful effect on the mind and body. Yet the evidence is indisputable. There's far more to good music than meets the ear. Wisely used, it can create a healthy and stimulating sound world for your family and profoundly enhance your child's growth.[13]

Do you remember Charlie Brown's teacher? Remember what she always said? "Wa-wa-wa wawa-wa-wa." No one knows what the poor woman was talking about because she was just talking and talking and talking! Now if she had been singing, we would remember.

As I said, I love the simplicity and wisdom of Mr. Rogers. If you have never watched his iconic children's programs I recommend them to you and your little ones. They may seem slow by today's standards, but they are profoundly educational, inspirational, and relational. You and your children will soon find yourself singing along in his neighborhood. Here are his thoughts on music:

> Music is the one art we all have inside. We may not be able to play an instrument, but we can sing along or clap or tap our feet. Have you ever see a baby bouncing up and down in the crib in time to some music? When you think of it, some of that baby's first messages from his or her parents may have been lullabies, or at least the music of their speaking voices. All of us have had the experience of hearing a tune from childhood and having that melody evoke a memory or a feeling. The music we hear early on tends to stay with us all our lives.[14]

LAW OF REQUISITE VARIETY

Did you take physics in high school or college? You may remember bumping into this: disequilibrium = life. This is the law of requisite variety. The survival of any system depends on its capacity to cultivate *variety* in its internal structures.[15] How does this apply to parenting? Simply put—mix it up! Take all those PattyCake Daily Ideas and add more of your own. Don't try to do them all in one sitting—try one a day as you practice connecting with your child or children. You will soon learn how they best respond, how they best learn, and what brings positive results.

Nicola Call writes, "Some children learn best by hearing, some by seeing and some by touching . . . remember to *mix it up* since a combination of styles makes a better 'glue.'"[16]

LET'S CELEBRATE

People love parties! Celebrating is a BIG deal and it is a big deal to God. Just think about the times He commanded His people to take vacations and have big dinners together. In the Bible, they are called "feasts" or "festivals," and there were seven of them during one calendar year.

Jesus's first miracle was at a wedding party. He made sure they had plenty of wine for celebrating. Celebrating is a good and healthy thing to do. It is especially effective in little lives. So don't wait until their birthdays or Christmas—find a reason now to rejoice!

- Potty-training
- First trip to the dentist
- A new baby in the family
- Starting school
- School is out
- Grew an inch
- Learned to ride a bike

- Learned to tie shoes
- Caught a ball ten times
- Learned a song
- Memorized a Bible verse
- Memorized the books of the Bible (They can do it! Use music.)
- Told someone about Jesus

Have you heard these words, **"Look, Mommy, I DID IT ALL BY MYSELF!"** YAHOO! Have a PARTY.

There is no end of creative ideas for celebrating. Here are some fun party/celebration ideas from my family life:

- Make cupcakes with a favorite color icing.
- Have a spur-of-the-moment parade.
- Dance and make up a silly song: "You tied your shoes, good for you! You tied your shoes, something new! YAY! Good for you!"
- Draw a picture of the event.
- Make a memory box and put in a token or scrap of something from the event/day/anwered prayer so you will remember.
- Make a T-shirt.
- Plant a tree or a flower.
- Establish a tradition.
- Create a proclamation: "Hear ye, hear ye, may it be known by all that _____ rode his bicycle all by himself today."

- When my daughter was five, she broke her arm so we had a cast party! Friends and family came to our house to sign her cast.
- Show your children how you celebrated them before they were born. Do you have pictures of a baby shower, gifts, preparing their room, baptism, and so on?

Don't forget to reward them for good things—obedience and achievement. God rewards our obedience both here and in eternity (See Matthew 5:12; Hebrews 11:6).

If you like to know you are doing things God's way (and I do), and you need some encouragement about a lifestyle of celebrating, check out this verse:

• •

Sing hymns instead of drinking songs!
Sing songs from your heart to Christ.
Sing praises over everything, any excuse for a song
to God the Father in the name of our Master, Jesus Christ.
EPHESIANS 5:19–20 (MSG)

• •

LAUGH A LOT
(Record your giggles before you forget!)

Our daughter was sitting in my husband's lap as he read a Bible story to her. She was looking at his face intently. He paused and said, "Isn't that a wonderful story? And God loves you just like He loved Daniel and took care of him in the lions' den."

Marilyn was gazing up and nodding. She said, "Daddy?"

"Yes, sweetheart."

"Why do you have hair in your nose?"

Thankfully I took the time to write that one in my journal. The look on my husband's face was priceless . . . he had no words. There are so many funny things I have forgotten and I am sad I didn't write about more of them or take pictures. In the moment these little events seem so large you think you could never *not* remember them. Like the day my son found my red nail polish and decided to paint his toenails, the bedspread, the carpet, and somehow the dog. He was three, and he was out of my sight for about ten minutes. I probably remember this moment over others since it cost us four hundred dollars to replace the rug. *Ugh.*

You may want to start a notebook or make a memory box for Fun and Funnies. Sad to say, these early years will be gone quickly. I have a notebook full of funnies sent to me, and from my own family. Here are a few of my favorites:

BIG GIGGLE BREAK

Garrett (age four): "Daddy, when I grow up
I want to be a doctor!"
Proud dad: "That's great, son."
Garrett: "Or maybe a dinosaur."

Melanie (age five) asked her granny how old she was.
Granny replied she was so old she didn't remember anymore.
Melanie said, "If you don't remember,
you just look in the back of your panties.
Mine say five to six."

. . . .

Steven (age three) hugged and kissed his mom good night.
"I love you so much that when you die
I'm going to bury you outside my bedroom window."

. . . .

Brittany (age four) had an earache and wanted a painkiller.
She tried in vain to take the lid off the bottle.
Seeing her frustration, her mom explained it was
a childproof cap and she'd have to open it for her.
Eyes wide with wonder, the little girl asked:
"How does it know it's me?"

. . . .

Clinton (age five) was in his bedroom looking worried.
When his mom asked what was troubling him, he replied,
"I don't know what'll happen with this bed
when I get married. How will my wife fit in it?"

. . . .

Susan (age four) was drinking juice when she got the hiccups.
"Please don't give me this juice again," she said.
"It makes my teeth cough."

James (age four) was listening to a Bible story.
His dad read: "The man named Lot was warned
to take his wife and flee out of the city,
but his wife looked back and was turned to salt."
Concerned, James asked:
"What happened to the flea?"

. . . .

Marc (age four) was engrossed in a young couple
who were hugging and kissing in a restaurant.
Without taking his eyes off them, he asked his dad:
"Why is he whispering in her mouth?"

. . . .

Marcus (my nephew, age four) ran into the surf
on his very first beach visit. A wave crashed over him
and he came up angry and sputtering.
With hands on his little hips he yelled,
"Mommy! Who put salt in this water?"

. . . .

A little boy eyed me after a concert in a church.
I was sitting in a chair in full Miss PattyCake costume.
His mother approached me, saying,
"Oh, he just loves you!
He watches you all the time on TV."
He hung back . . . he wasn't too sure about me.
I did my usual, "Hi there, what's your name?"
He said, "Are you a real, live, human person?"

Tammy (age four) was with her mother when they met an elderly, rather wrinkled woman her mom knew. Tammy looked at her for a while and then asked, "Why doesn't your skin fit your face?"

. . . .

Alice (my niece, age four) asked my mother if they could sing that song about hiking to heaven. No one was sure which song she meant until sometime later it began to play on a CD and she said, "That's it!" In the song, "Be Thou My Vision," the lyric is "High King of Heaven. . . . "[17]

. . . .

MY ALL-TIME FAVORITE:

The Sunday morning prayer I think this mom will never forget: "Dear Lord," the minister began, with arms extended toward heaven and a rapturous look on his upturned face. "We thank Thee that Thou dost remember that we are but dust. " He took a breath and would have continued, but at that moment her daughter leaned over and asked quite audibly in her shrill little four-year-old voice, "Mommy, what is BUTT dust?"

Chapter 7

IMPERATIVE—DO IT!

Do not merely listen to the word [of God],
and so deceive yourselves. Do what it says.

JAMES 1:22

My maternal grandmother was a strict Southern lady. She was formidable; no one crossed her, not even Gramps. He would just chuckle at her seriousness and say, "Isn't she cute?" She was famous for saying, "Dahlin', you should nevuh end your sentence with a prepuhzishun, and nevuh wear white aftuh Labuh Day." I miss her Southern drawl. She graduated from Judson College in Alabama, earned her master's in English at Columbia University in New York City, studied voice at Julliard School of Music in the 1920s, and that was somethin' else for a young, single woman from Montgomery, Alabama. In our family, she was the "language sheriff." I come by it generationally . . . my children call me a "grammar geek." I do not say everything correctly, but I fuss about it. So I feel qualified to give a lesson on a part of grammar: punctuation. Specifically, we're going to discuss the exclamation mark.

EX·CLA·MA·TION

noun \[ek-skluh-mey-shuhn]

: a sharp or sudden cry: a word, phrase, or sound that expresses a strong emotion

1. a sharp or sudden utterance
2. vehement expression.[1]

That is the technical name of the punctuation mark. Here is the type of directive it implies:

IM·PER·A·TIVE

adjective \[im-per-uh-tiv]

: very important grammar : having the form
that expresses a command rather than a
statement or a question: expressing a
command in a forceful and confident way.[2]

The use of an imperative means *Do it—not optional.*

Remember, "Hallelujah" is always followed by an exclamation point in the Bible. Flip your Bible open to the Psalms and see for yourself.

This imperative (!) chapter is written to prompt you into action:

Hebrews 10:24 (emphasis mine) says:

> *Let us consider how we may* spur *one another*
> *on toward love and good deeds.*

It is our job, our privilege, our responsibility, our joy to hear what God has to say, then **do it**! In an effort to spur you on, let's see what the Word of God has to say about teaching children and/or grandchildren about God, Jesus, and the Holy Spirit:

> *Keep his decrees and commands, which I am giving you*
> *today, so that it may go well with you and your children*
> *after you and that you may live long in the land*
> *the LORD your God gives you for all time.*
>
> DEUTERONOMY 4:40

• •

*Hear, O Israel! The Lord is our God, the Lord is one
[the only God]! You shall love the Lord your God
with all your heart and mind and with all your soul
and with all your strength [your entire being].
These words, which I am commanding you today,
shall be [written] on your heart and mind. You shall teach
them diligently to your children [impressing God's precepts
on their minds and penetrating their hearts
with His truths] and shall speak of them when you sit in
your house and when you walk on the road
and when you lie down and when you get up.*

DEUTERONOMY 6:4–7 (AMP)

• •

*Tell it to your children, and let your children
tell it to their children,
and their children to the next generation.*

JOEL 1:3

• •

*"As for me, this is my covenant with them," says the Lord.
"My Spirit, who is on you, will not depart from you,
and my words that I have put in your mouth
will always be on your lips, on the lips of your children
and on the lips of their descendants—from this time on
and forever," says the Lord.*

ISAIAH 59:21

· ·

*The secret things belong to the LORD our God, but the
things revealed belong to us and to our children forever,
that we may follow all the words of this law.*

DEUTERONOMY 29:29

· ·

*Whoever fears the LORD has a secure fortress,
and for their children it will be a refuge.*

PROVERBS 14:26

· ·

*Only be careful, and watch yourselves closely so that you
do not forget the things your eyes have seen or let them fade
from your heart as long as you live. Teach them to your
children and to their children after them.*

DEUTERONOMY 4:9

· ·

*All your children will be taught by the LORD,
and great will be their peace.*

ISAIAH 54:13

· ·

*The promise is for you and for your children
and for all who are far off—
for all whom the LORD our God will call.*

ACTS 2:39

• •

At that time Jesus said, "I praise you, Father,
Lord of heaven and earth, because you have
hidden these things from the wise and learned,
and revealed them to little children."

MATTHEW 11:25

• •

We will not hide them from their descendants;
we will tell the next generation the praiseworthy deeds
of the LORD, his power, and the wonders he has done.
He decreed statutes for Jacob and established the law in
Israel, which he commanded our ancestors to teach their
children, so the next generation would know them,
even the children yet to be born, and they in turn
would tell their children.

PSALM 78:4–6

Again, be encouraged that you are placed and privileged to parent. This is something you CAN DO. You can **share God's big love with little lives.**

So, as you diligently tell these little ones about God, be encouraged by these words:

Let's not get tired of doing what is good.
At just the right time we will reap
a harvest of blessing if we don't give up.

GALATIANS 6:9 (NLT)

• •

My dear brothers and sisters, be strong and immovable.
Always work enthusiastically for the Lord, for you know
that nothing you do for the Lord is ever useless.

1 CORINTHIANS 15:58 (NLT)

HALLELUJAH FOR THAT!

George Barna of the Barna Research Group has done much writing on families. In *Revolutionary Parenting*, Barna notes there are three dominant approaches to parenting currently operative in the United States:

- **PARENTING BY DEFAULT** is termed the path of least resistance. In this approach, parents do whatever comes naturally to them as influenced by cultural norms and traditions. The objective is to keep everyone—parent, child, and others—as happy as possible, without letting parenting dominate other important or prioritized aspects of the parents' lives
- **TRIAL-AND-ERROR PARENTING** is a common alternative. This approach assumes that every parent is an amateur, there are no absolute guidelines to follow, and the best parents can do is to experiment, observe outcomes, and improve based upon their successes and failures.

- **REVOLUTIONARY PARENTING** is the least common approach. Such nurturing requires the parent to take God's words on life and family at face value and to apply those words faithfully and consistently.[3]

Barna says, "Revolutionary parenting, which is based on one's faith in God, makes parenting a life priority."[4]

Let's consider again the Stephen Covey statement, "Begin with the end in mind."[5] If you are holding a precious baby, if you are chasing a toddler, if you never sit still with a "terrific two," if you are busy all day with a three-year old, if you are teaching Sunday school to a preschooler, if you are a grandparent of any of these ages, *you* have the privilege of helping shape a life for eternity!

A bit more encouragement on that from our friend, Mr. Rogers:

> Each generation in its turn is a link between all that has gone before and all that comes after. That is true genetically and it is equally true in the transmission of identity. Our parents gave us what they were able to give, and we took what we could of it and made it part of ourselves. If we knew our grandparents, and even our great-grandparents, we will have taken from them . . . too. All that helped to make us who we are. We, in our turn, will offer what we can of ourselves to our children and their offspring.[6]

GIGGLE BREAK

A mother was preparing pancakes for her sons, Kevin (age five) and Ryan (age three). The boys began to argue over who would get the first pancake. Their mother saw the opportunity for a spiritual lesson. "If Jesus were sitting here, He would say, 'Let my brother have the first pancake, I can wait.'" Kevin turned to his younger brother and said, "Ryan, you be Jesus!"

DO IT:
TELL THE GOOD NEWS

Tell your children about God, Jesus, the Holy Spirit, and the Bible. Find any way you can to bring God into conversations. It should be natural, organic, and it will get easier as you find simple ways to observe, then point your children to Him through creation, through situations, and though relations. I'll say it once more: music is an especially effective tool! Here are the lyrics from a song written for the Miss PattyCake Easter Eggstravaganza project.

1-2-3-4-5-6-7
Jesus made a way to heaven!
8 and 9 and then comes 10
Jesus died, then rose again.[7]

Sometimes the simplest answer works! The gospel is simple. Jesus did for us what we could not, cannot do for ourselves. No amount of trying harder, working, sacrificing, slaving, giving, being good, or any other form of effort is enough if we don't have Jesus. It's like Miss PattyCake's friend, Amazing Grace (an animated character who is a book in Miss PattyCake videos), says:

Well my dears, from the very beginning God wanted each one of us to be His very own child and live with Him forever. But because of our sin, you know, all the wrongs things we think and do, we could never be good enough no matter how hard we tried. But I'm so glad that God made a way.

The Bible says in John 3:16 that God loved the world so much that He sent His only Son, Jesus, to die on the cross. And whoever believes in Him will have life everlasting. You see, nobody loves you like God, and that's the truth![8]

I am not telling you it is easy to believe the gospel, but it is simple.

> From the very beginning God wanted each one of us to be His very own child and live with Him forever. . . . You see, nobody loves you like God, and that's the truth!

Jesus told the disciples that we should "become like little children" (Matthew 18:3). Children are dependent. They need us for everything. They can't eat, dress, clean themselves, find shelter, or stay safe without help. We should see ourselves like that. We need God's help for everything! Jesus said it well: "'I am the vine; you are the branches. . . . Apart from me, you can do *nothing*" (John 15:5, emphasis mine). This is the gospel—*the message*—the good news! Jesus did everything needed for us to know Him and live with Him forever.

Tell your children the good news. I'll help make it easier with the Miss PattyCake song, "Give Me Five He's Alive":

1. **Jesus was born**—He came to earth on Christmas morn.
2. **He loves you**—He lived a life so good and true.
3. **For you and me**—He gave his life on Calvary.
4. **There is so much more!** Three days later He *jumped* from the grave, then He went to heaven! And now, He prays for you and me . . . every day!
5. **He's alive—JESUS IS ALIVE!**[9]

When our daughter was four we were having sin problems. I mean, they started earlier than four, but at that age we were really working on obedience, good choices, doing the right thing, and thinking of others, because she was being selfish, disobedient, angry, and rebellious. Sound familiar? Ah yes, the human condition. I talked and prayed with her, reminding her to ask for God's help to obey. One day she actually said, "Mommy, I don't *want* to obey." There it is. The truth. And if we adults are honest, do we not all struggle with **wanting** to obey? Want some good news? Remember Philippians 2:13, "For it is God who is in you to *will* and to *act* in order to *fulfill* his good purpose" (emphasis mine.) We cannot **want** to obey without the Spirit of God working in and through us, and we need to ask for this grace daily. **The same is true for little children**. They need the same *good news*, the gospel: "For God so loved the world that he gave his one and only Son, that whoever believes in him shall not perish but have eternal life." (John 3:16)

The rest of my story is this: my little girl realized she needed help to obey. She also listened when I, and others, talked to her about being in God's "forever family." One day in her fourth year of life, all by herself, she prayed and asked Jesus to live with her and be her best friend. That was it! The miracle of new birth—she was a **believer**, and I noticed an immediate change. She became repentant, easily apologized, and mostly **wanted** to obey. I knew there was a difference in her little life! She had been infused with the spiritual DNA of Jesus and it changed her. She remembers it clearly and knows it was the moment she became a Christian. In case you think her decision may have been just a way to get me off her back, she has never strayed from her decision to follow Christ. I recall Dr. James Dobson, author, psychologist, and founder of Focus on the Family, telling the story of his own conversion experience at age three.[10]

> It is never too early to begin talking to your little one about this new life in Jesus.

It is never too early to begin talking to your little one about this new life in Jesus. Perhaps you will have the great privilege of leading your child, or any child, into a relationship with God through the Lord Jesus. Remember to be simple. Here is a sample prayer you might use:

Dear Father God, thank You for making me.
Thank You for loving me just the way I am.
Thank You for sending Your Son, Jesus, to live in our
    world, die on the cross, and take my punishment.
Thank You that Jesus didn't stay dead but came back
    to life! And thank You that Jesus made a way to
    heaven.
Forgive me for all the wrong things I think and do.
    Make me part of Your family so I can live with You
    forever. Fill my heart with Your love.
I ask you this in Jesus's name, amen. (Or maybe say
    YES, since that is what *amen* means.)

When this happens, **celebrate**! Have a party, call your family and/or friends, buy a new Bible and note the date, discuss a baptism. Do something to help your child know that Jesus said, "I tell you, there is rejoicing in the presence of the angels of God over one sinner who repents" (Luke 15:10). Since there is rejoicing in heaven, we ought also rejoice here on earth! **Celebration** is a good thing; **giving thanks** is a good thing; **praising God** is a good thing; **reading the Bible** and **praying** are good things. Then we are living every detail of our lives as Paul instructed: "Whatever you do, whether in word or deed, do it all in the name of the Lord Jesus, giving thanks to God the Father through him" (Colossians 3:17).

All these **good things** . . . remember what that sign at the mall said?

A CHILD'S MIND IS LIKE JELL-O.
THE IDEA IS TO PUT THE GOOD THINGS IN BEFORE IT SETS!

WRITE IT DOWN!

My daddy (aka Papa Roy) is famous in our family for these three words: "Write it down!" If we wanted something from him or tried to tell him something, his response was, "Write it down." Every day he wrote in a Day-Timer. Daddy, a brilliant and super organized engineer, developed and maintained systems that made my head spin. As the oldest of four children, I saw our house in constant motion—activities, church, school, clubs—and the only way to keep track of things was to write them down. To this day I follow my father's example; it has helped me a great deal.

King David wrote down his thoughts, questions, frustrations, praises, and revelations, and we have many Psalms because David journaled. Pastor Rick Warren says, "The spiritual habit of journaling is one that all Christians should understand and practice."[11] So write it down.

God said to Moses:

> *Write these commandments that I've given you*
> *today on your hearts. Get them inside of you*
> *and then get them inside your children.*
> *Talk about them wherever you are, sitting at home*
> *or walking in the street; talk about them*
> *from the time you get up in the morning to when*
> *you fall into bed at night. Tie them on your hands*
> *and foreheads as a reminder; inscribe them*
> *on the doorposts of your homes and on your city gates.*
> DEUTERONOMY 6:6–9 (MSG)

God knows that we forget stuff. First, He told us to write it down. Then He gave us other ways to remember. "Tie them on your hands [engrave them on bracelets] and foreheads [wear a hat, bandanna, headband with a scripture on it]"; "inscribe them on the doorposts of your homes [use a mezuzah or a wreath or plaque on the door with scripture] and on your city gates" [like on the walls of the Supreme Court].

Because of that biblical directive, and inspired by a trip to the great Saint Peter's Basilica in Rome where all the words of Matthew 16:18–19 are painted in enormous letters around the entire wall just next to the ceiling, I had an artist friend paint scripture in our home's entrance hall, living room, and kitchen. My husband and I carefully chose the verses we wanted on our walls. For us, these words are a daily reminder that God wants us to live joyfully!

Let the Word of Christ—the Message—
have the run of the house. . . .
Sing, sing your hearts out to God!
Let every detail in your lives—words, actions,
whatever—be done in the name of the Master, Jesus,
thanking God the Father every step of the way.
COLOSSIANS 3:16–17 (MSG)

Our favorite place in downtown Franklin, Tennessee is the Irish restaurant. The fish-and-chips are great! In addition to the food, the thing that draws me to this warm, noisy, friendly eatery is what is written near the ceiling around the narrow, long room. It's a portion of a lengthy poem, "The Breastplate of Saint Patrick," which, tradition says, he wrote in AD 433.[12] Patrick's written words have survived centuries and speak of his personal, close relationship with the Lord Jesus Christ. Patrick wrote these words as a prayer and included the real comfort he had found by inviting the presence of the Lord into every detail, just as Paul instructed above.

Christ be with me, Christ within me,
Christ behind me, Christ before me,
Christ beside me, Christ to win me,
Christ to comfort and restore me.
Christ beneath me, Christ above me,
Christ in quiet, Christ in danger,
Christ in hearts of all that love me,
Christ in mouth of friend and stranger.[13]

IS IT WORTH IT?

Did you know I'm related to a writer? You probably haven't heard of her, but she has written countless Bible studies, letters, notes, permission slips, menus, real-estate contracts, and poems. This fabulous woman has influenced my life from my earliest days and still does. Can you guess who she is? My mama, Bebe Herren Costner. I found this gem among her writings:

When my daughters, Jean and Lynn, were 4 and 3, a movie called *The Bible* came out. It began with the creation and went through Abraham and Isaac. Taking the girls was a treat, going to the big theater for their first time. Little did I know how frightening the last scene would be!

Abraham takes his only son up the mountain, ties him to an altar, and proceeds to raise the large, ugly knife over him. I heard Lynn gasp, making that sob sound just before the tears, and I quickly reached over Jean to calm her. Too late. I saw that Jean had already turned to her little sister and I heard her insistent voice as she loudly whispered, "It's okay, he won't kill him. I read the book."

What a moment! Not only was Lynn instantly soothed, but I was also given the deep reward all parents desire: Jean got it! All that time poured into the bedtime reading was worth it. I knew she could use what she had heard from the Bible in a real-life situation. It is a privilege to pass this on to encourage all you young mothers who struggle with the daily chores.

It's worth it. Just read the Book.[14]

So now you understand how I knew to tell my children early about God. My mother set a good example, and I am a *copy cat*. At this writing, my own children are twenty-two and twenty-three years old. I still talk to them about God all the time, just as my mother still talks to me about Him. (But they were grateful when I finally stopped singing Miss PattyCake songs at home.) I agree with my mother: it IS worth the effort of reading the Book.

One last imperative! I have taped these words to the shelf above my desk so I can read it often and remember my *why*. Why do I still put on the tights and green jumper? Why do I fly to places around the world and sing my simple songs? When I get weary, frustrated, or discouraged I lean into these strong words and remember that the work is alive and it is out in the world working. The little ones in your life are your work. The truth in these words motivates me to be a better mother, children's minister, coach, and encourager to anyone rearing, caring for, or working with little ones. Maybe you will want to make this your *why* and perhaps tape it to your mirror or refrigerator:

• •

The most significant aspect of every
person's life is his or her spiritual health.
We dare not neglect our role in spiritual formation,
which is the foundation upon which
their salvation and faith are built.
It is the best gift we can give
the children/grandchildren in our care.[15]

• •

YOU CAN DO THIS!

"I can do all things through Christ who strengthens me" (Phil 4:13 NKJV). Remember in the introduction when you spoke that verse out loud with me? It is *true* and God is with us! There it is again, that command with an exclamation point, an **imperative!** My editor says I use it way too much! She could be right. But God is so very serious about bringing little ones into the knowledge of His love that the extra exclamation points are necessary to bring attention to what He says. The good news—His gift of salvation through Jesus—can be received and believed in little lives! Then we will **give thanks with great joy** to the Lord, "for he has rescued us from the kingdom of darkness and transferred us into the Kingdom of his dear Son" (Colossians 1:13 NLT).

So let's recap about how PRAISE! can be instilled into little lives:

You have been Placed and Privileged to Parent.

You have a Rare Window of Opportunity.

You have an All-Access Pass to God and you hold the master key: PRAYER.

You know to begin in Infancy.

You have learned Seven Ways to Practice Praise.

You can do this with Enthusiastic Enjoyment.

And now you know it is Imperative!

Thanks for spending some time with me. Just now I am sitting at my kitchen table typing, praying for you and for the little ones in your life. I hope walking through a bit of my life, my experiences, and some of God's Word has given you new tools and enthusiastic confidence in God's ability to help you. **Sharing God's big love with little lives** is a high calling and great responsibility. I pray God will make your heart bigger with His love, and it will spill into every crazy moment of your life! Don't forget to **rejoice**, be **glad**, and **find the fun**.

Finally, as a fellow traveler and sister to you, I speak a blessing over you and the children in your care. I bless you in the beautiful name of the Lord Jesus. I come alongside to help hold up your arms as Aaron did for his brother, Moses (Exodus 17:12). And I speak to you these strong and living words:

· ·

May the Lord *bless* **you**
and protect **you**.
May the Lord *smile* **on you**
and be gracious **to you**.
May the Lord **show you** his *favor*
and give **you** his *peace*.

Amen

NUMBERS 6:24–26 (NLT)

· ·

ACKNOWLEDGMENTS

THANKS BE TO GOD! Little is much in Your upside-down kingdom, and You chose little me for this BIG work. Astonishing! Thank You for giving me a "garment of praise"—my life is JOYFUL!

Thanks to:

Chris Thomason for saying **yes** to the Miss PattyCake idea twenty-two years ago, and for continuing to be my partner in every way. You have labored countless hours designing products, marketing, working backstage, selling merchandise, running sound, booking travel, working on schedules, babysitting, encouraging me to keep going, videotaping all our children's events when I was on the road, and never minding your title, Mr. PattyCake. Our life together is colorful! I love you.

Nancy Gordon for cleverly crafting songs that led to the brilliant idea of creating a costumed character. Thank you for bringing your idea to me! Thank you for spurring me on "to love and good deeds." Your work is still working. YAY, GOD!

Karl Horstmann for seeing and sharing our vision, creating Miss PattyCake's world, and making her a "movie star!" You love children and love using your art form to reach little ones for God's kingdom. You will see your investment in eternity!

Marilyn and Christopher for making me a **mother** (not that you had a choice). You have made my life full—I love you BIG MUCH.

Mama (Bebe Herren Costner), my lifelong cheerleader and my ambassador. I have copied **you** in parenting and loving little ones. You are the original Miss PattyCake. I'm forever grateful God put me in your family. "The lines have fallen to me in pleasant places; indeed, my heritage is beautiful to me" (Psalm 16:6 NASB).

Daddy (Papa Roy Costner), fabulous father of mine! You are a grand grandfather and faithful servant of God, and you have modeled parenting so well. Thank you for always being my biggest fan! I will never be as great as you think I am, but I will always be a chip off the ol' block and proud of it. You have loved me well, and I am forever grateful.

Lynn Costner Farris and Sissy Costner Boone, my sisters. What would my life look like without you? I don't want to know! You have been Aaron and Hur in this project, and I have finished stronger because of you. We still have "miles to go before we sleep!"

Pappaw and Gamma (Earl and Brenda Thomason), grandparents extraordinaire! Thank you for loving our children so well and encouraging them in their personal faith. You have poured your time, energy, love, and faith into first your son, and now your grandchildren. I am grateful.

Deb Hash, my collaborator, editor, road manager, prayer warrior, stay-up-all-night-to-get-it-right FRIEND. You are faithful and true.

Sheryl Chernault. Thank you for thousands of road miles, years of encouragement, and all the times you said, "Write the book!" You are FABULOUS!

Kai Vilhelmsen, Mr. Stan the Handyman, singer, writer, actor, brother from another mother. You are AMAZERIFIC!

Ginnie Johnson, my regal, colorful friend! Your encouragement and collaboration helped me believe I could write a book. My life is brighter because I know you!

Dr. Mark Wyatt for saying YES that day I "accidentally" bumped into you in a bookstore in Mobile, Alabama. Thanks for taking on this project and telling me I am an author! God works in jots and tittles, widows and orphans.

All brothers and sisters involved in children's ministry: You have welcomed me into your churches, ministries, festivals, conferences, camps, parades, carnivals, parties, holiday celebrations, hospitals, homes, and hearts. I have grown and learned from all of you. I am grateful. #kidmin

Joyfully,

Jean

NOTES

INTRODUCTION

1. Nancy Gordon and Chris Springer, "Pattycake Praise" (Nashville: Integrity's Hosanna! Music, 1994). Hosanna! Music (ASCAP) adm. at CapitalCMGPublishing.com. All rights reserved. Used by permission.

CHAPTER 1: Placed and Privileged to Parent

1. Lila Empson, *Soul Retreat for Moms* (Grand Rapids: Inspirio/Zondervan, 2002).
2. Twila Paris. *Kingdom Seekers*. StraightWay Music, ASCAP, a Division of Jubilee Communications, Inc, WR 8303, 1985, Vinyl LP.
3. Ann Voskamp. *One Thousand Gifts* (Grand Rapids: Zondervan, 2010).
4. F. B. Meyer, *The Secret of Guidance* (Chicago, IL: Moody Publishers, 2010).

CHAPTER 2: Rare Window of Opportunity

1. Julia Cameron, *The Artist's Way for Parents* (New York: TarcherPerigee, 2014), 4.
2. "Favor." *Merriam-Webster Dictionary*. Accessed December 1, 2016. https://www.merriam-webster.com/dictionary/favor.
3. Clare Herbert Woolston, "Jesus Loves the Little Children." Public domain.
4. David Whitehead, *Making Sense of the Bible: Rediscovering the Power of Scripture Today* (Bloomington, MN: Bethany House Publishers, 2014).
5. Darlene Schacht, *Teach Them Who God Is*. www.timewarpwife.com. February 18, 2013.
6. George Barna, *Transforming Children into Spiritual Champions* (Ventura, CA: Regal House Publishing, 2003).
7. Ibid.
8. Urban Child Institute, *Baby's Brain Begins Now: Conception to Age 3*. www.urbanchildinstitute.org. April 18 2011, emphasis mine.
9. Zero to Three: National Center for Infants, Toddlers and Families, *Brain Development*. www.zerotothree.org.
10. Paul Reisser, *Complete Guide to Baby & Child Care* (Wheaton: Tyndale House, 1997). Emphasis mine.
11. R. S. Lee, *Your Growing Children and Religion* (New York: Penguin Books, 1967).
12. St. Ignatius of Loyola, Founder, Society of Jesuits. 1539. https://en.wikipedia.org/wiki/Ignatius_of_Loyola.
13. George Barna, *Transforming Children into Spiritual Champions* (Ventura, CA: Regal House Publishing, 2003).
14. Forest E. Witcraft, Scholar/Teacher, "A hundred years from now . . ." http://www.values.com/inspirational-quotes/4244-a-hundred-years-from-now-it-. Jan. 23, 2014.
15. Dave Stone, *Raising Your Kids to Love the Lord* (Nashville: Thomas Nelson, 2013).

16. "Discipline." *Merriam-Webster Dictionary*. Accessed December 1, 2016. https://www.merriam-webster.com/dictionary/discipline.

17. Katherine Lee, *Surprising Reasons Why We Need to Discipline Children*. http://childparenting.about.com.

18. Helen Young, *Children Won't Wait: Sharing the Precious Moments of Your Baby's Childhood* (Ft. Worth, TX: Brownlow Publishing, 1995).

CHAPTER 3: All-Access Pass

1. James Strong, *The New Strong's Exhaustive Concordance of the Bible* (Nashville: Thomas Nelson, 2010), #8085.

2. Max Lucado, *Before Amen* (Nashville: Thomas Nelson, 2016).

CHAPTER 4: Infancy

1. As quoted in Elisa Morgan and Carol Kuykendall, *What Every Mom Needs* (Grand Rapids: Zondervan, 1995).

2. Elisa Morgan and Carol Kuykendall, *What Every Mom Needs* (Grand Rapids: Zondervan, 1995).

3. Plato, "You know that the beginning . . .." *Republic*. 380 BC. https://en.wikipedia.org/wiki/Republic_(Plato).

4. Jeanne Hendricks, (speech, MOPS International Leadership Convention, 1994).

5. Patti Chadwick, *Lois and Eunice*. www.historyswomen.com. PC Publications, 22 Williams St., Batavia, NY 14020. www.pcpublications.org.

6. Stephen R. Covey, *The Seven Habits of Highly Effective People,* rev. ed. (New York: Simon & Schuster, 2013).

7. Dr. Billy Graham, (excerpt from commencement address at Liberty University, Lynchburg, Virginia, on May 3, 1997); http://billygrahamlibrary.org/from-billy-graham-to-the-graduate/.

CHAPTER 5: Seven Ways to Practice Praise

1. Jack R. Taylor, *Hallelujah Factor*, rev. ed. (Mansfield, PA: Kingdom Publishing, 1999).

2. Marsha B. Edelman, "Cantillation: Chanting, or Leyning, the Bible." *My Jewish Learning*. http://www.myjewishlearning.com/article/cantillation-chanting-the-bible/.

3. Dr. Bruce Leafblad, "Biblical Principles for Music Ministry" (lecture, Southwestern Baptist Theological Seminary, Dallas, TX, 1985), emphasis mine.

4. M. G. Easton, *Illustrated Bible Dictionary* (New York: Cosimo Classics, 2005).

5. Graham Kendrick, ed., *The Source: v. 2: The Worship Collection* (Buxhall, UK: Kevin Mayhew Ltd., July 2001).

6. Ibid.

7. Ibid.

8. William Carruthers, *Westminster Shorter Catechism of the Westminster Assembly of Divines*. November 25, 1647 (1st Edition); http://www.opc.org/sc.html.

9. Catherine Marshall, *Something More*, rev. ed. (Ada, MI: Chosen Books, 2002).

10. See Mark 15:38; Matthew 27:51

11. Jack R. Taylor, *Hallelujah Factor*, rev. ed. (Mansfield, PA: Kingdom Publishing, 1999).
12. Ibid.
13. Ann Voskamp, *One Thousand Gifts* (Grand Rapids: Zondervan, 2010).
14. Belden C. Lane, *Ravished by Beauty: The Surprising Legacy of Reformed Spirituality* (Oxford: Oxford University Press, 2011).
15. Pascal, Blaise. *Pensées*. published posthumously, 1670.
16. Ann Voskamp, *One Thousand Gifts* (Grand Rapids: Zondervan, 2010), emphasis mine.

CHAPTER 6: Enthusiastic Enjoyment

1. "Enthusiasm." *Online Etymology Dictionary*. Accessed December 1, 2016. http://www.etymonline.com/index.php?term=enthusiasm&allowed_in_frame=0.
2. "Stress Management." *Mayo Clinic*. Accessed December 1, 2016. http://www.mayoclinic.org/healthy-lifestyle/stress-management/in-depth/stress-relief/art-20044456.
3. Marilyn Meberg, *I'd Rather Be Laughing* (Nashville: W Publishing Group, 1998).
4. Robert B. Sherman and Richard M. Sherman. "A Spoonful of Sugar." Walt Disney Records. Copyright: 1964.
5. Steve Merkel and Jean Thomason, "Colors, Numbers, ABCs" (Nashville: Integrity's Hosanna! Music, 2002). Hosanna! Music (ASCAP) adm. at CapitalCMGPublishing .com. All rights reserved. Used by permission.
6. Julia Cameron, *The Artist's Way for Parents* (New York: TarcherPerigee, 2014), 12-13.
7. Nancy Gordon and Rhonda Scelsi, "Copy Cat" (Nashville: Integrity's Hosanna! Music, 1995). Hosanna! Music (ASCAP) adm. at CapitalCMGPublishing.com. All rights reserved. Used by permission.
8. Claire Cloninger and Nancy Gordon, "Hullabaloo" (Nashville: Integrity's Hosanna! Music, 1994). Juniper Landing Music (ASCAP) adm. at Word Music, Inc. All rights reserved. Used by permission.
9. Don Campbell, *The Mozart Effect for Children* (New York: William Morrow/HarperCollins, 2000).
10. Ibid.
11. "30 Awesome Music Quotes from Famous Non-Musicians," Plato, *MyMusicMasterClass.com*, (blog), https://www.mymusicmasterclass.com/blog/30-awesome-music-quotes-from-famous-non-musicians/.
12. Don Campbell, *The Mozart Effect for Children* (New York: William Morrow/HarperCollins, 2000).
13. Ibid.
14. Fred Rogers, *The World According to Mister Rogers* (New York: Hyperion, 2003), 18.
15. Mark Batterson, *Wild Goose Chase* (New York: Multnomah Books, 2008), 62.
16. Nicola Call, *The Thinking Child: Brain-Based Learning for the Early Years Foundation Stage,* 2nd ed. (London: Bloomsbury Academic, 2010).
17. Mary E. Byrne, translator, "Be Thou My Vision." *Hymnary.org*. http://www.hymnary.org/text/be_thou_my_vision_o_lord_of_my_heart.

CHAPTER 7: Imperative—Do It!

1. "Exclamation." *Meriam-Webster Dictionary*. https://www.merriam-webster.com/dictionary/exclamation.

2. "Imperative." *Meriam-Webster Dictionary*. https://www.merriam-webster.com/dictionary/imperative

3. Barna, George, *Revolutionary Parenting* (Carol Stream, IL: Tyndale Momentum, 2007).

4. Ibid.

5. Stephen R. Covey, *The Seven Habits of Highly Effective People,* rev. ed. (New York: Simon & Schuster, 2013).

6. Fred Rogers, *The World According to Mister Rogers* (New York: Hyperion, 2003), 54.

7. Steve Merkel and Jean Thomason, "Colors, Numbers, ABCs" (Nashville: Integrity's Hosanna! Music, 2002). Hosanna! Music (ASCAP) adm. at CapitalCMGPublishing .com. All rights reserved. Used by permission.

8. Steve Merkel and Jean Thomason, lines for animated character "Amazing Grace" (Nashville: Integrity's Hosanna! Music, 2002). Hosanna! Music (ASCAP) adm. at CapitalCMGPublishing.com. All rights reserved. Used by permission.

9. Nancy Gordon, Steve Merkel, and Jean Thomason, "Give Me Five, He's Alive" (Nashville: Integrity's Hosanna! Music, 2002). Hosanna! Music (ASCAP) adm. at CapitalCMGPublishing.com. All rights reserved. Used by permission.

10. Alan S. L. Wong, "Different Philosophies of Child Evangelism," vtaide.com, http://www.vtaide.com/gleanings/child-evangelism3.htm.

11. Rick Warren, "The Spiritual Act of Journaling," *Pastor Rick's Daily Hope,* December 11, 2014, http://pastorrick.com/devotional/english-with-tags/the-spiritual-act-of-journaling#.WEGWeXeZPFw.

12. "Saint Patrick's Breastplate," *PrayerFoundation.org,* http://www.prayerfoundation.org/st_patricks_breastplate_prayer.htm. Public Domain.

13. Ibid.

14. Bebe Herren Costner, journal entry, May 2005, emphasis mine.

15. George Barna, *Transforming Children into Spiritual Champions* (Ventura, CA: Regal House Publishing, 2003).

ABOUT THE AUTHOR

JEAN THOMASON has more than 30 years of experience as a musical performer, worship leader, author, and conference speaker to parents, grandparents, teachers, and children's ministers. She is the living embodiment of the joyful children's musical character, "Miss PattyCake." Through this brightly costumed character, Jean plants biblical truths, broken into fun, toddler-size pieces, while helping equip parents to lay a spiritual foundation for their children. Her live "Miss PattyCake" family events are performed throughout God's great big world.

For more information,
visit www.misspattycake.com.

@PattyCakePraise   Facebook.com/   Youtube.com/   @Jean_Thomason
@JeanThomason3   pattycakepraise   misspattycaketv

For Speaking or Concert Booking Inquiries:
friends@misspattycake.com

This biblically based resource kit is filled with hands-on, guided activities. It can be easily adapted by Homeschool Groups, church preschools, preschool choirs, VBS, and more!

The fun songs will connect with your children, creating fertile ground for the Word of God to be planted deep within their hearts.

As you use these songs, activities, and scripted programs, your little ones will learn about the love of God and be drawn toward a life-long faith in Him.

You can trust this material to:

- Have a solid Biblical foundation.
- Give a practical, working plan.
- Teach age-appropriate music.
- Offer lots of fun in the learning!

You can find this resource on: misspattycake.com

Get the entire collection!

misspattycake.com

Rent or Download Videos
misspattycake.pivotshare.com

IF YOU ENJOYED THIS BOOK, WILL YOU CONSIDER SHARING THE MESSAGE WITH OTHERS?

Mention the book in a blog post or through Facebook, Twitter, Pinterest, or upload a picture through Instagram.

Recommend this book to those in your small group, book club, workplace, and classes.

Head over to facebook.com/worthypublishing, "LIKE" the page, and post a comment as to what you enjoyed the most.

Tweet "I recommend reading #SharingGodsBigLove by @PattyCakePraise // @worthypub"

Pick up a copy for someone you know who would be challenged and encouraged by this message.

Write a book review online.

WORTHY®
PUBLISHING

Visit us at worthypublishing.com

twitter.com/worthypub

worthypub.tumblr.com

facebook.com/worthypublishing

pinterest.com/worthypub

instagram.com/worthypub

youtube.com/worthypublishing